USING THE BEST-SELLING NOVEL TO SHARE YOUR FAITH

FEAR NOT *Da Vinci*

USING THE BEST-SELLING NOVEL TO SHARE YOUR FAITH

FEAR NOT *Da Vinci*

SUSY FLORY AND GINI MONROE
WITH W. WARD GASQUE, PhD

Fear Not Da Vinci: Using the Best-Selling Novel to Share Your Faith

Published by Living Ink Books, an imprint of AMG Publishers
6815 Shallowford Rd.
Chattanooga, Tennessee 37421

ISBN 0-89957-052-6
First printing—March 2006
Cover designed by ImageWright, Chattanooga, Tennessee
Interior design and typesetting by Reider Publishing Services, West Hollywood, California
Edited and Proofread by Rosemary Dupras, Dan Penwell, Sharon Neal, and Rick Steele

Printed in Canada
11 10 09 08 07 06 –T– 6 5 4 3 2 1

To Robert, my husband and my coach.
To my father, Frank Srubar, who loved God above all
and shared his faith with many.

SUSY

* * *

To my best friend and lifelong companion,
John, my husband.

GINI

Contents

Fear Not: Join God Where He Is Working

Foreword

DAN BROWN'S *The Da Vinci Code* has sold over forty million copies in more than forty-four languages, and there is no sign of its soon demise. Although the book is fiction, many gullible readers, some of them professing Christians, take it as historical fiction based on careful research.

And with Ron Howard's *Imagine Entertainment* and Tom Hanks in the starring role, the movie means that many more millions will be exposed to its controversial story line. This impending blockbuster opens the door for churches to discuss the faith in a manner that has been matched recently only by Mel Gibson's *The Passion of the Christ*.

Contrary to the suggestions of the popular press, Christians have nothing to fear from this book, but they do need to be critically informed. *Fear Not Da Vinci* gives them the tools to engage in an intelligent conversation with people who have read the book or seen the movie.

I hope many churches will use this book as a bridge to people who are outside of the faith.

W. Ward Gasque, PhD
Historian

Preface

ENTER *THE DA VINCI CODE*, the best-selling novel of all time. And now, thanks to the movie, *The Da Vinci Code* is here to stay. Many Christians judge the story to be an attack on the faith. Instead, we contend that it provides a unique and compelling opportunity for culturally relevant evangelism.

When we first read the book we got angry, but then we decided to do something. In the fall of 2004, we created a fun, interactive seminar to answer the spiritual questions raised in Dan Brown's novel. Our vision has since grown to include this book to encourage and equip you to use *The Da Vinci Code* to share your faith.

Fear Not Da Vinci recounts stories of *The Da Vinci Code*—encounters based on true events. Because we know these methods work, we challenge you to try them! May God encourage and strengthen you as you embark on what might be the most exciting adventure of all—sharing your faith.

Acknowledgments

MY DEEP THANKS to those who caught the vision for this book and who encouraged us, prayed for us, and nudged us along. Thank you Mark, Tracy, Larry, Brent, Mike, Tyler, Randy, Jason, Karen, Bruce, Margaret, Gayle, Dianne, Jon, Carol, Amanda, Diane, Kristy, Janet, Vivian; the wonderful women I work with at Neighborhood Church; the women of Reading Connection; and those who bravely attended our first *Da Vinci Code* seminar. The staff at a Christian Leaders, Authors & Speakers Services (CLASS) seminar played a key role in encouraging us in this project, along with a small but mighty prayer warrior we encountered there named Kelly. Dr. Gasque, thanks for your encouragement. And, to Robert, Ethan, Theodora, Mom, Sara, Jerry and Alice, you lift me up.

A special thanks to our dear editor, Dan Penwell, and the AMG publishing committee—first, for seeing the need for the book, and second, for shepherding it with care. Then Gini and I ask: how do other authors survive without an editor like Rosemary Dupras and a proofreader like Sharon Neal? These two ladies know everything, and we are grateful for their keen eyes and sharp pencils.

—SUSY

* * *

I thank Susy for continuing to encourage me to keep writing. Thank you, John, for your insight and constant love. Thanks to Rob, Lisa, Reed, Hollie, Kathy, Becki, Charlotte, the 11:30 Women's class, and Misti and Martha, who prayed unflaggingly for us. Thanks to Diane and Margie for following and staying close to Jesus.

But mostly, thank you Lord for allowing us the joy of carrying your truth and name. Be glorified, Lord. This is your book!

—Gini

Introduction

The Da Vinci Code *Dare*

"Fear not . . ."

—LUKE 5:10 (KJV)

I HAVE A DARE for you! Find a copy of *The Da Vinci Code*. Tuck it under your arm and carry it around for a few days. When you ride the bus or take an airplane, set the book on your lap. When you visit a store, set it on the counter while you pay. When you go to the park and sit on a bench, open it up and pretend you're reading. Don't flash it around or wave it under people's noses. Just tote it around for a few days.

If you take the dare, people will begin to talk to you. People you've never met, people you may never see again, people who are very different from you.

An unexpected connection

Not long ago, I was in the airport to catch a flight to Chicago. My copy of *The Da Vinci Code* was hidden away in a large tote bag with some magazines, my day planner, and a bottle of water. Then a red light flashed and I was herded over to the line for an extreme security check, the kind where you take your shoes off and an uncomfortable looking woman pats you down, opens up your bags, and touches everything.

"How are you today?" The security official's badge read FRAN. She looked tired, eyes distant.

"I'm okay." I shrugged my shoulders up and tilted my head down, trying to release the tension in my neck. I wondered if I had anything sharp in my bag, like a nail file or safety pins.

Fran finished going through my purse and turned to my tote bag. She opened my day planner, replaced it carefully. Then she saw it. *The Da Vinci Code.*

Quick Facts: The Controversy

The Da Vinci Code claims . . .

- Jesus married Mary Magdalene.
- Jesus and Mary had a child.
- The bloodline survived in France.
- The Roman Catholic Church conspired to hide the truth.
- Roman emperor Constantine hatched the idea that Jesus was divine.
- Leonardo da Vinci hid clues to these mysteries in his artwork.

A huge smile spread across her face. Her eyes sparkled as she held the book up. "I read this book."

I couldn't help but smile back. "It's a good story."

"I love it! I stayed up late reading it for four nights. My husband had to sleep with a pillow over his eyes."

We grinned at each other, tickled by the unexpected connection. Then she took a last look at the red and gold cover, peering down into the eyes of Mona Lisa.

Fran carefully slid the book back inside my bag, then rested her hand on top. "I can't wait 'til the movie comes out."

She was still smiling as she waved the next passenger up to her station.

Why don't I talk to strangers?

Now, let me make a confession. I don't talk to strangers. This is embarrassing because believers are supposed to be friendly, full of love, charity, and compassion, reaching out with the message of Christ to a lost and dying world. However, I've found this hard to do since I don't talk to strangers.

Maybe it's just plain selfishness. I have my own agenda, my own plans for the day, and I don't like to be interrupted. Most times I don't notice the tired mom in front of me at the grocery store. I walk too quickly into the bank to smile at the three-year-old playing with his toy car on the floor. I'm too busy thinking of my next errand to chat with the dry cleaner.

Or maybe it's fear. It's scary to talk to people you don't know, to open up and share yourself for a few minutes. It's hard to meet their eyes, to connect. My heart beats hard, my tongue gets tangled, I'm silent.

Then again, could it be discomfort at recognizing the gulf between us? After all, I know Jesus, I've tasted truth, and they haven't. I have no clue how to start to cross that gulf; I don't know what to say or how to share.

Yet, not talking to strangers seems wrong. Am I sinning when I ignore people, when I don't connect, when I surrender to fear or when I'm distracted by my own plans and my own needs? God calls us to be salt and light and to share the truth with our generation: "Woe to me if I do not preach the gospel!" (1 Cor. 9:16).

Take the dare

So how does someone like me, and maybe like you—scared, busy, uncomfortable, and unprepared—reach out and share our hearts with strangers? How do we connect with people who need what we have?

Take the dare!

Carry the book around for a week and see what happens, who talks to you, and what questions they ask. People are passionate about this book and this movie, and you will connect.

CHAPTER

ONE

The Buzz

Who cares? It's just a novel.

"Send forth your light and your truth."

—PSALM 43:3

NOT LONG AGO, I was sipping a latte with a friend. "I just read this new book called *The DaVinci Code*," she said.

We were sitting at a café table, lazy in the sun. But something in her voice, an aliveness, an intensity, caught me. She looked straight into my eyes. "It explained so many things for me."

Millions sold

As I write these words, forty million hardback copies of *The Da Vinci Code* are in print. To put those numbers in perspective, a book is considered a best seller with just 100,000 copies sold. (I'm smiling as I write "just 100,000 copies" because most writers would love to have those sales figures attached to their books.) Dan Brown's three other novels, once almost unknown, are now also best sellers.

Since its release in 2003, *The Da Vinci Code* has dominated the best-seller lists not only in the United States but also in Australia,

England, Italy, France, Hong Kong, Ireland, Holland, China, Slovenia, Canada, Russia, and Singapore. According to the media, *The Da Vinci Code* is now the best-selling fiction book ever.[1] What an eyebrow-raising statistic, especially since as I write this, the paperback version has not yet been released. It's anyone's guess where the sales figures will top out now that the less expensive paperback version is available in every grocery store.

Da Vinci Code Tourism

- "Cracking *The Da Vinci Code*," by Paris Muse. We begin at the Arc du Carrousel for a brief fifteen-minute walking tour of the area around the Louvre. We then enter the Louvre for a two-hour art tour featuring Leonardo da Vinci.[2]
- "*Da Vinci Code* London," by British Tours Ltd. Choose a three- or seven-hour tour. Follow in the footsteps of Langdon and Neveu, featured in Dan Brown's best-selling novel *The Da Vinci Code*.[3]
- "*Da Vinci Code* Tour," by Chateau de Villette, France. A publishing phenomenon, Dan Brown's #1 best-selling novel *The Da Vinci Code* featured Villette as the residence of his character Sir Leigh Teabing, a British royal historian who, at Chateau de Villette, revealed the secrets of the Holy Grail and the relationship of Jesus and Mary Magdalene. Includes 6 days/5 nights deluxe room at Chateau de Villette.[4]
- "On the Trail of *The Da Vinci Code*," by Beyond Boundaries Travel. This scavenger hunt through France and England will explore symbology and codes in art in a unique way while giving trip participants the chance to experience the thrill of the "hunt." The nine-day tour begins on October 9 and includes four nights in Paris, three nights in London, and one night in Edinburgh.[5]

- "Da Vinci Pilgrimage," by Sacred Journeys for Women. We will travel into the mysterious world of *The Da Vinci Code* with the unparalleled guidance of an expert in the field of alternative history—Simon Cox, best-selling author of *Cracking The Da Vinci Code*. This will be an amazing inner journey, an opportunity to bring the bigger questions of your life to the surface and delve deeply into your own meaning of the feminine divine.[6]

The movie

The Da Vinci Code movie release date is May 19, 2006. Ron Howard (*Splash, Apollo 13, A Beautiful Mind*) is directing and Brian Grazer producing. Tom Hanks stars as hero, Robert Langdon, and Audrey Tatou plays the beautiful cryptologist, Sophie Neveu. Locations include the Louvre Museum in Paris as well as Scotland's Rosslyn Chapel. Westminster Abbey refused to give the filmmakers permission to shoot scenes in the one-thousand-year-old church where British royalty is crowned and buried; instead, Lincoln Cathedral (in Lincolnshire, England) stands in for the Abbey. A British nun held a prayer and protest vigil outside Lincoln Cathedral and was reported to have confronted Tom Hanks on his way to the set. "To a believer, any believer, what is happening is blasphemous," said Sister Mary Michael in an interview.[7]

In 2001, the same Ron Howard/Brian Grazer team produced *A Beautiful Mind.* The film starred Russell Crowe and won four Academy Awards, including Best Picture and Best Director. Howard and Grazer teamed with Akiva Goldsman, who won an Oscar for best screenplay. The film racked up $312 million in ticket sales.

A Beautiful Mind tells the true story of John Nash, a brilliant but asocial mathematician who accepts secret work in cryptography. His life takes a turn to the nightmarish in a film that's been called "a beautiful mystery."

Like *The Da Vinci Code* film, *A Beautiful Mind* is adapted from a successful book—*A Beautiful Mind: The Life of Mathematical Genius and Nobel Laureate John Nash* by Sylvia Nasar—features the talent of the Howard/Grazer/Goldsman team, and takes the audience on a thrill ride with twists, turns, and loads of intrigue. Ron Howard is no stranger to controversy, either. *A Beautiful Mind* was criticized for changing the book and leaving out crucial facts about the subject's life, such as his homosexuality and his frequent adulterous affairs.

> "I won't read the book, but I'll probably watch the movie version. And that's only because I'm a big fan of Tom Hanks."
>
> —Actress Bea Alonzo, a devout Catholic who said she deplores the subject matter of the book[8]

All this to say that Howard knows how to manage controversy to his advantage, as well as how to put together a talented team able to sell legions of movie tickets and rake in major awards. Like *A Beautiful Mind, The Da Vinci Code* will likely also be an entertaining and controversial film, earning hundreds of millions of dollars and dozens of awards. When movie ticket sales slow, a year or two after its initial release, a new furor will kick up when *The Da Vinci Code* video/DVD appears in stores. Later, one of the big three TV networks will feature the film in prime time.

The movie reaches a previously untapped fan base for *The Da Vinci Code* success story—children. In the past, Tom Hanks and Ron Howard have proven to be family favorites with Hanks films like *Big* and *Forrest Gump*, and Howard movies like *Apollo 13, Backdraft*, and *Cocoon*.

The impact

In addition to the movie, *The Da Vinci Code* has spawned nearly a dozen documentaries. Innumerable magazine articles, book reviews, and blog posts have also tackled the *Code*'s mysteries. Even gamers get their chance to unlock the code with video games from 2K Games, as well as several mobile games from Kayak Interactive. Kayak's president explained: "The *Da Vinci Code* story engages the audience and makes them think both through the ongoing story itself and through a variety of puzzles that are solved by the characters throughout. In terms of a game design, these are all great features to base game play on."[9]

The Da Vinci Code has also bred a whole mini-industry of best-selling *Da Vinci Code* books, which generally fall into two categories: (1) readers' guides, which explore the minutiae of the people, places, artwork, and history mentioned in the book, and (2) debunkers, which critique the history and theology of the novel. If you enter the words "Da Vinci Code" into any online bookstore search bar, it will bring up the titles of more than eighty books written in response to the novel.

College Courses Based on *The Da Vinci Code*

- "Da Vinci's Code," Sweet Briar College, Virginia. The course examines the authenticity, truth, plausibility, and validity of the novel's claims in the context of Renaissance art and culture.[10]
- "*The Da Vinci Code*," University of Tasmania, Australia. *The Da Vinci Code*'s assumptions will be examined from a cultural and historical point of view.[11]
- "A Cracking Course for Fans of *Da Vinci Code*," Newbattle Abbey College, Newbattle, Scotland. Students will try to unravel the mystery of *The Da Vinci Code*. They will study the carvings at Rosslyn Chapel in the village of Roslin, which inspired Dan Brown's thriller and which many believe contain secrets of the Holy Grail.[12]

- "*The Da Vinci Code*," Northwestern State University of Louisiana, Natchitoches, Louisiana. *The Da Vinci Code* opens up all kinds of fascinating questions about the formation of the early Christian Church and the role of the sacred feminine in religion, especially the role of Mary Magdalene.[13]

I threw it against the wall

After the latte with my friend, I went home and ordered a copy of *The Da Vinci Code* to see for myself exactly what it had explained to my friend. When it arrived, I couldn't put it down. An engrossing piece of thrill writing, *The Da Vinci Code* whisks readers away on a journey through Paris and London with a Harvard professor and a French cryptologist who struggle to decipher codes and solve puzzles leading to the true identity of the Holy Grail.

When I got to page 238, I finally saw what all the fuss was about. "Almost everything our fathers taught us about Christ is false," announced a main character. A few pages later, the hero claims "every faith in the world is based on fabrication. That is the definition of faith—acceptance of that which we imagine to be true, that which we cannot prove."

I closed the book. Thought awhile. Then threw it against the wall.

Was this the same book my friend had talked about over coffee? I was confused. We had gone to Christian school together, prayed together, even studied the Bible together. How could she believe this stuff?

I was angry, angry enough to put a dent in the wall, because *The Da Vinci Code* lies. I was angry because it was so entertaining. And I was angry because my friend believes it's true.

Overheard: Common Responses to *The Da Vinci Code*

"It nearly made me lose my faith."

"It's just a novel."

"It shows that the Bible can't possibly be accurate and that the text was changed."

"It made me question everything."

"It made me think I don't have any real facts to back up my faith."

"I want to know more. I want to know if it's all true."

"The book is true or it couldn't be printed."

"While the book is 'fiction,' one can't help but believe much of it."

The Christian response

So far, in responding to the book and the movie, Christians tend to fall into one of three groups:

1. The majority, who have not read the book and are unaware of the impact of *The Da Vinci Code*.
2. Those who have read the book and perceive it as a nice little piece of entertainment, although they may not agree with its claims.
3. Those who, like me, are angry or confused by the claims of the book and the film. This last group may even judge the book as a deliberate attack on their faith.

When I first read *The Da Vinci Code* after the conversation with my friend, I definitely fit into that last group—aware of and angry at a book that attacked the very foundations of everything I believe.

Unaware

But many Christians are unaware of the book or at least the historical claims that it makes. The Barna Group, Christian pollsters, reported in a recent study that only 18 percent of Protestants have read *The Da Vinci Code*, compared to 40 percent of American Catholics. The study reported: "The book also drew many readers from those who are aligned with a faith other than Christianity and from those who are atheists and agnostics. Self-described liberals were more than twice as likely as those who portray themselves as conservative to have read the book."[14]

When I asked a Christian friend, an avid reader, why she refuses to read *The Da Vinci Code*, she gave two reasons: "I don't know the whole story, but I've heard it's full of falsehoods, so why read it? Also, I don't want to support the author with my money by buying his book."

I can see her point. Jesus himself has called us to be a city on a hill in Matthew 5:14, separate and unblemished from the world and its corruption. If *The Da Vinci Code* is corrupt, then it makes sense to avoid reading or buying it, except that it can't be completely avoided. With forty million copies of the book currently in print, chances are, as you read these words, there's a copy somewhere nearby. Now with the movie and its accompanying advertising campaign, no one, not even my cautious friend, can avoid the discussion.

So the question becomes, can you discuss *The Da Vinci Code* without having read the book or watched the film? Maybe in a vague, philosophical sort of way. Remember when the first Harry Potter book came out? Christians were outraged at the presence of the occult in the best-selling book. The debate raged, with Christians on either side of the "read or don't read" fence. At the height of the debate, a close friend read *Harry Potter and the Sorcerer's Stone*, loved it, and wanted to talk about it. I was curious and guarded, having heard some of the uproar. In particular, Christians were quoting Deuteronomy 18:10: "Let no one be found among you who sacrifices his son or daughter in the fire, who practices divination or sorcery, interprets omens, engages in witchcraft." With that verse as ammunition, I met with my friend to debate the merits of Harry Potter. Her first question was "Have you read it?" I had to admit that I had not. Guess what? The discussion was over.

Unconcerned

Although many Christians have refused to read *The Da Vinci Code*, there are those who read it and enjoyed it. Many report reading through the book in a couple of days, mesmerized, unable to put it down. A small group leader at my church said, "I loved it. It was a great ride!" A Christian schoolteacher said that she loved the settings in the book, particularly Paris. "I just went to the Louvre last year on a trip, and it was exciting to read this adventure set in places that I've visited." At a party, a friend reported that she loved the adventure in the book. She dismissed the controversy with this: "If people actually believe the book's claims about Jesus are true, then they probably believe *The National Enquirer* is true, too."

Christians are consumers and are not immune to well-crafted entertainment like *The Da Vinci Code*. "This is a thriller for people who don't like thrillers. It's tremendously engaging as a reading experience, while at the same time, you are learning something," explained Stephen Rubin, publisher of *The Da Vinci Code.*[15]

Perhaps the author himself, widely quoted in the media with his stock phrase, can best sum up the broad appeal of *The Da Vinci Code*: "Everybody loves a conspiracy."

But what about my friend, the one who told me *The Da Vinci Code* explained "so many things"? I can't just dismiss her. She read it, she loved it, and she believed it. And she's smart enough not to believe grocery store tabloids.

In *Decoding Da Vinci*, author Amy Welborn argues that Christians should not underestimate the book's cultural impact: " 'It's only a novel,' some folks say. 'Everyone knows it's fiction. So why not just enjoy it on that level?' Well, there are several reasons why we can't do that. First, there is no such thing as 'only a novel.' Culture matters. Culture communicates. We should always be interested in the content of culture and its impact on us, no matter if we're talking about art, film, music, or writing."[16]

Christians need to stay in touch. By monitoring what people are looking at, listening to, and reading, we can gain some understanding of what they are thinking and what they believe. Then we can open the discussion.

Unprepared

There is a third group—Christians who have read *The Da Vinci Code* and have not liked it, appalled by its inaccurate historical claims and attacks on Christianity. I'm in this group. *The Da Vinci Code*'s runaway popularity makes us want to throw our books against the wall and argue against it. We may even have read the debunkers and we're ready with Bible verses to beat down the opposition. Pause. We are missing something: the culture is fascinated with Jesus and his true identity. People wonder if the Bible can be trusted and if their faith is built on facts. They question everything from Jesus' marital status to the intentions of Leonardo da Vinci's paintings and even God's gender. Should we answer? Scripture says yes: "Make the most of every opportunity . . . so that you may know how to answer everyone" (Col. 4:5, 6).

People are looking for purpose and for truth, even in best-selling novels. "The popularity of both the book and the [TV] special points to our culture's continuing fascination with Jesus," writes Darrell Bock, author of *Breaking The Da Vinci Code*. "And even when that curiosity borders on the perverse, we need to be engaged in the conversation—if not on TV specials, certainly in our neighborhoods, schools, and offices, wherever the topic of conversation comes up—talking about the real Jesus in a constructive way."[17]

We need to be ready to enter the discussion over a book that is a confusing mix of truth, half-truths, and untruths. "Dan Brown begins the book by laying out what he calls historical facts," said Bart Erhman, author of *Truth and Fiction in The Da Vinci Code*, "and he includes the statement that all descriptions of art, architecture, sacred rituals, and documents are factual. The difficulty I had reading through *The Da Vinci Code* with that in mind was that most of the descriptions of ancient documents, in fact, are not factual—they're part of his fiction. But people reading the book aren't equipped to separate the fact from the fiction."[18]

Needed: A guide

Most people who read *The Da Vinci Code* are just everyday people like you or me, not scholars, historians, or college professors. And most people today don't know much about the Bible. So how can they know what is true and what is not? Bock calls the faith questions in *The Da Vinci Code* "largely unknown territory for readers of the novel. One needs a guide for the terrain. The issues of faith and relationship to God are too important to be left to the confusing category of 'historical' fiction."[19]

The fictional discussions of *The Da Vinci Code* characters illuminate a fresh curiosity arising in our culture. Researcher Scott Thumma calls this an "era of seekership . . . Many Americans—and not just the young ones—are perusing the religious landscape and trying to choose on an individual level what they want to believe, like chemists mixing and matching compounds in a spiritual experiment."[20]

Who will be the guide to this tricky terrain? Who will light the way as seekers look for truth? Many of us have spent countless hours reading and studying the Bible, and we know who Jesus really is. We know the power and the love of a personal relationship with the Son of God. The guide? It's us—we must carry the light. We need to talk to our curious neighbors, our friends, our relatives and realize that, perhaps, *The Da Vinci Code* is part of God's plan. Perhaps Jesus will use *The Da Vinci Code* to call the curious to a deeper knowledge of him. Perhaps the book and the movie will stir up a longing for the truth.

Rather than throw *The Da Vinci Code* against the wall, we can throw it into the "all things" category in the biblical promise of Romans 8:28: "And we know that in all things God works for the good of those who love him, who have been called according to his purpose." We can defend the faith by sharing the faith through quiet conversation, asking thoughtful questions, and gently nudging *Da Vinci Code* fans away from the "*Da Vinci Code* Jesus" to the real Jesus.

A Prayer

God, I'm just a regular person and I'm not sure what I can do to reach out to people who are intrigued by *The Da Vinci Code.* Give me a heart for those who are searching for truth, and the strength to learn what to say. Use me to help carry the light of the gospel to those who are in the dark. Thank you that you can use a book and movie like *The Da Vinci Code* to call people to yourself. Amen.

CHAPTER
TWO

The Challenge

Is it okay to read The Da Vinci Code?

"... by all possible means ..."

—1 CORINTHIANS 9:22

THE DA VINCI CODE is a fun, crazy best seller. It intrigues people. It raises questions about faith, about who Jesus is, and about where the Bible comes from. The book has impacted our culture, and it's impossible not to notice the buzz.

If you haven't yet read *The Da Vinci Code*, chances are your friends and neighbors have. Your colleagues are buzzing about it. Your kids are dying to see the movie. Your cousin wonders if it's true. It's time for you to decode Da Vinci.

Shari says it's full of lies

If you take the dare, and carry the book around for a few days, you'll get your share of friendly smiles, and you'll connect and chat—but probably not at church. I haven't had the guts to schlep the book around at church, but I have talked about it and there are no smiles or friendly chats. Christians are alarmed by the very mention of it; this became clear during a conversation at my Bible study.

Before we start the study, everyone hangs out by the kitchen counter pouring coffee, making tea, and nibbling on pretzels. I had just finished *The Da Vinci Code* and was dying to talk it over with friends.

"I just read the most intense book. I couldn't put it down." I stirred some cream into my coffee.

"What was it?" Amy turned towards me, eyebrows up.

"*The Da Vinci Code*."

Everyone in Bible study froze, straining to hear me. It was quiet, just like when my cats hear a strange noise. They freeze, stuck in some random weird position. Nothing moves except their ears, which swivel around and point towards the noise. Apparently, I was the strange noise.

"I heard that book was full of lies," Shari announced from the sofa. "It's an attack on the faith. I would never read something like that."

Heads nodded in agreement. Amy tilted her head. "So what did it say? What's *Da Vinci Code* about?"

"Jesus was married to Mary Magdalene and had kids." Shari spoke with venom. "Can you believe it? What a piece of trash."

"I got about two-thirds of the way through it and got so mad I threw it straight into the garbage," Renee chimed in, folding her arms across her chest.

My face grew warm. The conversation was over. I still wanted to discuss the claims in the book, but I didn't want to stir up any more angry responses among my friends.

Were they right? Is *The Da Vinci Code* trash? Should believers read it or throw it out? Is it right or wrong to support the author by buying his book or seeing the movie?

Quick Facts: *The Da Vinci Code* Phenomenon

- The best-selling novel of all time, with over forty million in print
- Ranked in the top ten on the New York Times Best Seller List for more than two years
- Translated into forty-four languages; a hit in Europe and Australia
- Author was recently named one of the world's one hundred most influential people by *Time* magazine
- Movie releases May, 2006, with Tom Hanks starring and Ron Howard directing

Reading *The Da Vinci Code* won't send you to hell

It's been promoted as a theological thriller, and it well deserves both parts of the nickname. A page-turner, it's thick with puzzles, symbols, cliff-hanging chapter endings and schemes by shadowy evil figures (see appendix A for a plot synopsis). But reading it is an uncomfortable pleasure; many believers hesitate to read it for fear of what God will think.

God says to keep our minds on what is pure and what is lovely (Phil. 4:8) when so much of what our culture offers is tainted and ugly. *The Da Vinci Code*, which questions the truth of the Gospel accounts of Jesus, could easily, and maybe even rightly, be judged as "trash." What's a believer to do?

Paul tackled a similar dilemma when he wrote to believers in the idol-filled city of Corinth. These new Christians wanted to know how they could live godly lives in an ungodly culture (1 Cor. 8:1–8).

Corinthian believers were arguing over whether to eat meat that had been sacrificed to idols in temples dedicated to pagan gods and goddesses. The people of the city brought offerings of food to priests at the temples. Some of the food was burned, some was eaten by the priests, and some was taken back to be eaten at feasts or even sold in the marketplace. Corinthian believers wondered if they could eat this meat with a clear conscience. Although the meat itself was good to eat, the question remained—had the meat been spiritually tainted by being sacrificed to a false god?

Now Christians face a similar dilemma: is it wrong to read this book or see the movie? *The Da Vinci Code* offers an entertaining story but contains clear attacks on the Christian faith, angering many believers. How did Paul deal with the similar dilemma in Corinth?

Read it . . . or not?

1. Paul cautions against hasty choices. Believers live in community, and the decision to read a controversial book will be noticed by those around us. Consider the matter soberly and recognize that only God knows the best course. "Now let's talk about food that has been sacrificed to idols. You think that everyone should agree with your perfect knowledge. Anyone who claims to know all the answers doesn't really know very much" (1 Cor. 8:1, 2 NLT).

What Can I Do? Pray before you take the *Da Vinci Code* dare. Consider your own level of spiritual maturity. Do you have trouble evaluating competing ideas of faith? Then *The Da Vinci Code* dare may not be for you. Do not judge either those who choose to read it, or those who do not; God directs. (Be forewarned: The book contains some violence and one brief description of a supposed ancient sexual rite.)

2. Physical actions such as eating spiritually tainted meat do not affect our standing with God. "Food does not bring us near to God; we are no worse if we do not eat, and no better if we do" (1 Cor. 8:8).

What Can I Do? Know that the action alone of reading a book like *The Da Vinci Code* will neither condemn nor save you. Deciding to follow Christ is an issue of the spirit and the will, not of outward behavior.

3. To reach out to those in our culture, believers may choose to become familiar with popular cultural practices in order to build a bridge to discuss questions of faith. "Though I am free and belong to no man . . . I have become all things to all men so that by all possible means I might save some" (1 Cor. 9:19, 22).

What Can I Do? It might be a good idea to read *The Da Vinci Code* or see the movie so that you can talk about the spiritual claims and issues. Perhaps this will serve as a unique chance to share your faith with people who are searching.

4. However, believers must carefully examine their motives against Paul's principle that our actions should have a greater purpose: winning others to Christ. "I do all this for the sake of the gospel, that I may share in its blessing" (1 Cor. 9:23).

What Can I Do? Assess your motives through prayer and advice from wise and godly people. If God allows you to move forward with a clear conscience, do so boldly, always "for the sake of the gospel."

5. God can use *The Da Vinci Code* for his purposes. What may have been written to achieve fame, to earn money, or to sow doubt can be turned around and used for good, if God chooses. Hank Hanegraaff, host of the *Bible Answer Man* radio program, explains: "Strange as it may seem, heresy has always been good for the church, since it forces a renewed attention to the central doctrines of Christianity in order to counteract error."[21]

What Can I Do? Don't worry about where the money goes. Some Christians wonder if it's okay to support this author by buying his book, but if you have worked through the decision prayerfully and have a clear conscience, go ahead and buy a copy of the book or a movie ticket. Scripture is clear: "The earth is the Lord's, and everything in it" (1 Cor. 10:26). Even *The Da Vinci Code* belongs to the Lord. The money you spend for the book or ticket belongs to the Lord. View the purchase as a few dollars well invested for the purpose of opening a door to share your faith. Or you can always try the library!

Rather than looking down on those who read *The Da Vinci Code* or enjoy the movie version, use it instead as a God-provided opportunity to talk to your friends, neighbors, and even strangers about spiritual things. What is meant for evil can sometimes turn out for good when God is at work.

The Da Vinci Code college

If you've been interested in *The Da Vinci Code* for a while, you may have read some of the books debunking it. Historians and theologians have unearthed reams of errors while deconstructing and disproving the "facts" in the novel. Some authors critique the book from a Christian point of view, while some use a strictly historical view. What most of the debunking books have in common is an academic tone with authors who possess advanced degrees. You don't need a string of initials after your name to talk to people about *The Da Vinci Code.* But if you're considering taking the dare to share your faith, then you do need to "prepare your mind for action" (1 Pet. 1:13).

First, read the book or see the movie. When fans make a point to chat with you, they'll be disgusted if you're completely ignorant of the story.

Next, note the spiritual claims, especially as related to Leonardo da Vinci's artwork, Jesus, Mary Magdalene, and the Bible. These four topics seem to produce the key questions that arise over and over. If you own a copy of the book, take a pen and circle or star these areas. Fold the corner over so you can go back later.

Last, it's time for *Da Vinci Code* college. The book you hold in your hand will prepare you to use *The Da Vinci Code* to share your faith. First, we offer some thoughts on why and how to share your faith. Next, we'll share effective strategies for using *The Da Vinci Code.* Then, we'll introduce you to several different scenarios you might encounter including a five-minute chat on the subway; a dinner party conversation; an art lesson for kids; and a letter to a close relative. The scenarios include specific questions you're likely to encounter, along with satisfying answers (many from the academic sources mentioned earlier). We'll also direct you to helpful resources to further equip you for your task.

All you need to do is to be willing to take the dare and we'll help you with the rest. Is God calling you to share your faith? Do not be afraid, "for God has not given us a spirit of fear, but of power and of love" (2 Tim. 1:7 NKJV). *The Da Vinci Code* is a bridge to the culture—let's cross it together.

CHAPTER
THREE

The Reason

Why should I share my faith?

"I try to find common ground with everyone so that I might bring them to Christ."

—1 CORINTHIANS 9:22 (NLT)

MY FAMILY generally doesn't allow me into candy stores. They're simply too dangerous for a confirmed chocoholic like me who spends way too much time and money on dark chocolate. But there is one place I can enjoy my passion for chocolate without harassment—my local warehouse store.

Cleanup on the candy aisle

With my shopping cart loaded with soda, dog food, and toilet paper, I navigate through the crowded aisles of the warehouse store towards the checkout stands. But first I always stop at the candy aisle and scan the brightly colored bags and wrappers, searching for something new, rich and intriguing.

On one of my recent shopping trips my cart was loaded down with bags, bottles, and boxes bulging from every inch of the cart. I tried passing by the candy aisle, but something caught my eye—stacks of gold-boxed Godiva chocolates. I picked up a box. Enraptured by the metallic wrapping and the promise of luxury within, I didn't notice the oncoming cart.

"Ex-kah-uze me," a harried-looking lady snapped, speeding her cart past mine. I smiled, steered my cart a bit closer to the side, and then got back to the chocolate.

Out of the corner of my eye, I saw another cart approach. *Careful . . . you're too close . . . you're never going to make it . . . watch out!* Too late. Upon impact my cart jerked, there was a ripping sound, and the box of chocolates flipped out of my hands and landed on the floor, where it quickly disappeared under the dog food trickling out of the torn bag under my cart.

"Oh, sorry!" the speeding cart driver said. He was middle aged, with a gray ponytail and deep smile lines around his eyes. "I am really sorry. I'll go find someone to clean this up."

"It's okay," I said. "After all, I was kind of hogging the entire aisle." I bent over to pick up the Godivas. I stood looking at the box, trying to decide if I should splurge.

"Hey, you know, those mixed chocolates are pretty good, but the truffles are even better." The Ponytail Guy grabbed the handle of his cart and tried to work it loose.

"I've never tried the truffles." I held my cart steady as more dog food trickled to the floor. "They're a little richer, right?"

"No, they're a lot richer. Wait 'til you try the amaretto. It'll make your taste buds sing!" He nudged at the pile of dog food, trying to rake it over to the side with his shoe. Then he smiled, eyes crinkling. This man knew his chocolate.

"All right. You have my mouth watering," I agreed. "I'll be right back." I left, planning to find a new cart so I could abandon the dog food and transfer over the rest of my groceries.

When I returned a few minutes later, I noticed something new on top of my old cart—a small gold box of Godiva truffles with a $10 bill folded over the top. SORRY FOR THE MESS was written in neat black letters around the edge of the bill. ENJOY!

Wow, this guy must have really liked this chocolate to buy a box for a complete stranger. You have to admire that kind of passion, that drive to share something you love with someone who doesn't know.

Guess what? When I got to the car I opened that golden box and had a couple of Godiva truffles before I even started the engine. And they were just as he said—incredible.

I wonder. What are Christians like when it comes to sharing our faith? Do we appreciate what we have? Do we look for interest? Do we radiate excitement and passion? Are we ready when we find chances to talk? Do we share our personal experiences, even in quick, simple moments at the store or the park or at work? Do we give our faith away, like Ponytail Guy gave me a box of the chocolates he loved?

Grace and Godiva chocolate

In the early years of the church, the passion for God's truth was contagious. After Jesus left, the church grew from just a few hundred people to more than 500,000, all within one generation. The Good News of Jesus' gift of eternal life ignited and spread rapidly, with new people added daily to the family of believers. What program did they use? The Ponytail Guy's. Here it is:

1. Hang out where other people hang out. The Ponytail Guy was out shopping in the warehouse store, rolling down the candy aisle. You can't meet people and talk to them if you don't go where they go. Sometimes Christians are surprised by this philosophy. Here's a story from one man who decided to take a yoga class. While a popular form of exercise, yoga is rather controversial for Christians. Here's his rationale for participating: "[I take yoga] because there are no Christians there; because some teachers practice Buddhism and chant in class; and because although I am not tempted to believe what they say or act upon it, others in the class are." When a friend complained that he spent more time with non-Christians than Christians, he explained: "Of course, if there were more Christians doing these activities, I wouldn't be alone!"[22]

What Can I Do? Make a point of mixing with unchurched people in your community by joining a club, taking a class, or even just taking your dog for a walk. You can't share your faith if you don't meet unbelievers. Jesus spent time with people in their homes, in the fields, at town centers, and on the beach: "The Son of Man came eating and drinking . . . 'a friend of tax collectors and sinners' " (Matt. 11:19).

2. Observe what people are interested in. Although he ran into my cart by accident, the Ponytail Guy was alert enough to notice my box of chocolates, and he even recognized the Godiva packaging.

What Can I Do? Make a point of noticing what your friends and coworkers are reading, watching, and talking about. If you don't recognize a title or author, ask a few friendly questions. Keep an eye out for those who read books, like *The Da Vinci Code,* which delve into spiritual matters. A new interest in spiritual topics just might mean that God is at work in someone's heart. In the book, *Get the Word Out,* the author explains that "seekers have tasted something of God, and their lives have begun to manifest a deeper hunger for God himself."[23]

3. Ask a question or make a comment to gauge the level of interest. Ponytail Guy observed aloud that I was holding mixed chocolates and mentioned that he liked the truffles. If I had gathered up my groceries and run away, he probably would have concluded that I wasn't that interested in the chocolate. If I had briefly agreed and turned my back, the conversation would have ended. However, when I asked if the truffles were richer in flavor, then he knew I was really interested in the chocolate.

What Can I Do? Have a few questions ready to start a deeper conversation with a seeker. Jesus often used questions when he talked with his followers and encountered seekers. "Who do you say that I am?" he asked the disciples (Mark 8:29). A little later he asked the rich young man, "Why do you call me good?" (Mark 10:18). Some simple conversation deepeners include:

- How are things going for you?
- Do you think much about spiritual things?
- How can I pray for you?
- What do you think about God?
- What gives meaning to your life?

4. Share your own experience. Ponytail Guy had purchased Godiva truffles before, loved them, and even described the flavor of the amaretto truffle. The details of his own experience helped to convince me that he knew what he was talking about.

What Can I Do? Practice your own faith story. How did you come to follow Jesus? What was your life like before? What is your life like now? Emphasize the change in your life and your sense of purpose. Then make it clear that anyone can experience that same change if they choose to follow Jesus. He is the answer to life's most difficult problems. "The gospel speaks directly to the human situation as can no other truth. Whether or not people will admit their desperate need of reconciliation, it is actually everyone's deepest longing."[24]

5. Show your emotions. Be excited and enthusiastic when you talk about your faith. Ponytail Guy loved chocolate and showed that by his enthusiasm, his smile, and his attention.

What Can I Do? Spend time in worship every morning. Center your thoughts on Jesus and what he has done for you. Cultivate an attitude of thankfulness and ask God to give you a spirit of joy and warmth for all to see.

6. Lastly, give something away. In our consumer culture, we expect strings attached to everything. When you fill out an entry form for a car giveaway, you expect to get a phone call selling timeshares. When a guy washes your windows at a stoplight, you expect him to ask for money. No one gives anything away for free, except a Ponytail Guy. He gives away Godiva chocolates.

What Can I Do? When you meet someone who shows an interest in Jesus, give something away—a box of chocolates, a book or a CD, or perhaps a latte and an hour of your time. "People crave attention . . . It becomes the connecting bridge between them and God. Best of all, instead of asking them for something—their time, attention, and interest—we give them something—our time, attention, and interest. We serve them a small taste of Jesus' desire to attend to them."[25]

A friend told me of a recent mission trip to China where he and his team taught conversational English. A turning point in the trip came when the Chinese students realized that the American team consisted of unpaid volunteers. Why would the Americans take time off work and pay large amounts of their own money to come all the way to China to teach English? A wave of surprise and confusion rippled over the class as, for the first time, the students understood the sacrifice. Wide-eyed, their faces softened into smiles. The room remained quiet. Hearts were opened for the team to go on and share a little about Jesus and his sacrifice.

People take notice of free gifts and they treasure unselfish acts. Free gifts are unexpected. Shocking, even. They serve as a tangible illustration of God's grace—undeserved, but freely given.

Grace

"As your understanding of the impact of God's grace in your own life grows, learning how to communicate that to the unbeliever is paramount. Grace is what changes people. Seeing the result of it in others is what draws people to seek grace for themselves. Your story of grace is the miracle that will change lives."

—From *Permission Evangelism* by Michael Simpson

You will be my witnesses

If someone could get so enthusiastic over a small box of chocolates, how much more passionate should we be about our new life with Jesus? The last instruction Jesus gave before ascending to heaven was to share the Good News in his Great Commission in Matthew 28:19, 20: "Therefore go and make disciples of all nations, baptizing them in the name of the Father and of the Son and of the Holy Spirit, and teaching them to obey everything I have commanded you. And surely I am with you always, to the very end of the age."

Like giving testimony in a court case, witnesses are expected simply to report the facts of what they have seen and experienced. And thankfully, Jesus promises help from the Holy Spirit in this joyous task of serving as his witness: "But you will receive power when the Holy Spirit comes on you; and you will be my witnesses in Jerusalem, and in all Judea and Samaria, and to the ends of the earth" (Acts 1:8).

What does a witness do?

- ***Witnesses report.*** I have a friend, Joan, with problems and struggles like anyone else. Yet there is a light about her and people notice. A checkout clerk at the grocery store recently asked, "How come you're always so happy? Why are you always smiling?" She simply answered, "Because I know the Lord." She is a witness; she reports what she has experienced.
- ***Witnesses share.*** Jan loves to talk about her sustaining faith. When people find out that she is completely blind, the questions begin. "What happened to your eyes?" or "How long have you been blind?" Sometimes people get more personal and ask things like "How do you put on your makeup?" But Jan doesn't mind; instead, she uses the questions as an opportunity to connect. "My overall strategy is to open my mouth, wherever I am and whoever I'm with, no matter what the situation. I use my tragedy to share God's love and peace." She

often asks, "May I share what Jesus has done for me?" Jan is a witness; she makes herself vulnerable and shares her story with anyone who will listen.

- ***Witnesses worship.*** When she first began sharing her faith, Carole Brewer, a professional singer, was often nervous. "To overcome fear, I've prayed for boldness and God has given it to me. I've learned that God has put footprints on the floor, and I just step into them." Carole is a witness; she sings about what God has done for her.

Backed by God

The process of evangelism, from beginning to end, is dominated by God. Our role in winning the world is actually rather small. But our role is critical. Will we live sent, filled, and followed? Will we get the word out?

—From *Get the Word Out* by John Teter

- ***Witnesses go out.*** Robert had never been on a mission trip before when he was invited to travel to Cuba as part of a church team. He worried about the dangers of traveling to a third-world country and the possibilities of disease and food poisoning. He worried about leaving his family. He worried about raising enough money. He worried about his own physical problems. But he prayed and afterward felt strongly that he should go. He was afraid, but he went anyway. While in Cuba, he had the privilege of helping several children pray to receive Jesus. Robert is a witness; he was afraid and felt unworthy, but he went. A witness goes out into the world.
- ***Witnesses love people.*** Jason became friends with a guy he met at work. His friend was troubled and Jason worried about him.

One day at lunch, Jason said to his friend, "You know, I care about you and I just really feel like I have to share with you about Jesus. Will you listen?" His friend listened and decided to follow Jesus. Jason is a witness; he loves his friend and wants the best for him.

- ***Witnesses want to please God.*** Since God offers a way for all to be saved, he sends out his witnesses to share this wonderful news. Paul puts it this way: "We speak as men approved by God to be entrusted with the gospel. We are not trying to please men but God, who tests our hearts" (1 Thess. 2:4). A few years ago I was at a memorial service for a motorcycle cop who was killed in the line of duty. Hundreds of motorcycle police officers showed up to pay their respects. I was seated next to some rough looking ex-police officers in leather vests embroidered with skulls, knives, and dripping blood. One of these Hells Angel–type guys was friendly and we began to talk. I asked him what the insignias on his vest meant, and several had religious meaning. I was a little confused by his rough demeanor, and I think he could tell. Then he surprised me. "When I go up to the sky and face the Big Guy, all I want is for him to look at me and say, 'Well done, my good and faithful servant.' " His answer cut me, and I wept. The rough and scary motorcycle guy is a witness; his primary goal is to please God.

Becoming a *Da Vinci Code* witness

We please God when we share him with people. Would you consider being a witness? Using *The Da Vinci Code* is just one way to share your faith; there are others. And the work has already started. Because evangelism, simply, is connecting with people in a place and a time where God is already at work in their lives. "People who have not yet embraced Jesus are on a journey. Someone has described the journey as going from zero to one hundred on a scale. Zero is completely in the dark and far from God. One hundred is accepting Jesus fully and falling deeply in love with him. Most people are somewhere between zero and one hundred. The goal? Push them a few points down the road."[26] Today would you try to push the people you meet just a point or two further? Maybe they will meet another Christian who will move them a couple more points and then, in a while, they will finally fall deeply in love with Jesus.

Unexpected Connection

Have you recently experienced a random act of kindness? Did someone unexpectedly connect with you? In your journal, write a description of the incident, along with a sentence about how you felt afterward. Next, try out the Ponytail Guy Method today at the gym, grocery store or at work. Notice someone, interact with them, and give them something for free. You can do it!

CHAPTER

FOUR

The Help

I don't know how to share my faith.

"Be prepared . . ."

—2 TIMOTHY 4:2

HAVE YOU EVER sent e-mail to someone by accident? I have. Although it was awkward and embarrassing, over the next few days an interesting conversation developed. Here's what happened:

From: *Susy*
To: *Martina, Danielle*
Sent: *Monday, October 24*
Subject: *The trip . . .*
Hey, Martina & Danielle! It looks like our weekend away is FINALLY going to happen. Dave was able to rearrange his work schedule and he's agreed to watch the kids. I found a great price online for a flight to Chicago. This is it! Are you ready for us, Martina?
Love ya,
Susy

***From:** Martina*
***To:** Susy, Danielle*
***Sent:** Monday, October 24*
***Subject:** Ready for a girls' weekend!*
*I am more than ready. It's been so lonely here. I've already been here three months, if you can believe it. And you two are my very first houseguests! I can't wait for you to see my apartment. And there's a great breakfast restaurant nearby called **Toast** that serves cinnamon waffles.*
Ciao,
Martina

***From:** Danielle*
***To:** Martina, Susy*
***Sent:** Monday, October 24*
***Subject:** Waffles, yum!*
***Toast** sounds great, Martina. I say let's stay out of the kitchen and eat out as much as we can. I've heard Chicago has great restaurants, and I want to personally investigate and see if it deserves that reputation! By the way, Martina, is there a church we can visit on*
Sunday?
Yours,
Danielle

***From:** Martina*
***To:** Susy, Danielle*
***Sent:** Monday, October 24*
***Subject:** Beyond food . . .*
*Danielle, don't worry. There are tons of great restaurants. **Toast** is only the beginning. And don't faint, but I've also been researching churches. There's a big one nearby called Woodside. It sounds nice.*
Ciao,
Martina

***From:** Susy*
***To:** Danielle, Martina*
***Sent:** Tuesday, October 25*
***Subject:** Re: Beyond Food . . .*
Danielle, can you believe it? Martina has been checking out churches!! I'm excited! I have been praying for her for so long. She stopped going to church back in college and I think she's been living a pretty wild life. Maybe God is working on her heart. I want so much for her to know his peace and love. And I want to see her in heaven. Let's agree together to pray for her as she searches, okay?
Love ya,
Susy

***From:** Martina*
***To:** Susy*
***Sent:** Tuesday, October 25*
***Subject:** Whoops—I don't think you meant for me to see this . . .*
Dear Susy:
I don't think I was supposed to receive that last e-mail. I'm guessing it was meant just for Danielle, but you sent it to me, too. This is a little awkward . . . but don't feel embarrassed! You are right—I haven't been to church in a long time. I know there is a spiritual void in my life. I believe in God, but I just feel like I don't really know where he is. You and I haven't actually ever talked about this. I guess I wasn't sure where to start.
Ciao,
Martina

***From:** Susy*
***To:** Martina*
***Sent:** Tuesday, October 25*
***Subject:** My face is sooo red!*
Dearest Martina:
I am so embarrassed! I thought I was going to die when I read the

first line of your e-mail and I realized I sent the e-mail to Danielle and TO YOU!!! Thank you for being so nice. I guess my defense is that Danielle and I do care about you and we truly want you to be happy.
Love ya,
Susy

From: *Martina*
To: *Susy*
Sent: *Wednesday, October 26*
Subject: *You're sweet*
Susy, you are a great friend. Don't worry about the e-mail. Really—it's okay. But now that we're on the subject, I have a question for you. You seem like you have it all together. I mean, you're peaceful and calm and you seem to take things in stride. You're kind, too. But I'm not. I get really angry when things don't go my way and I take it out on people. There are other things in my life that you don't even know about—things I'm really ashamed of. So, here's my question. I know what you were like in high school. You did your share of partying and fooling around. You could be pretty wild. How did you change? Because I'm not sure I can.
Ciao,
Martina

From: *Susy*
To: *Martina*
Sent: *Wednesday, October 26*
Subject: *It started with a book*
Martina, you're right. I've done some things I'm not proud of. I've been selfish and I've used people. I said I loved God, but I just lived for pleasure and I felt very empty. Then one Sunday my pastor challenged us to read through the Bible in a year, and I decided to go for it. It took me longer than a year, but you want to hear something strange? It changed me. The Bible is different from any other book I've ever read (and that's saying a lot, because you know what a bookworm I am)!
Love ya,
Susy

***From:** Martina*
***To:** Susy*
***Sent:** Thursday, October 27*
***Subject:** HOW is it different?*
Okay, Susy, you have my attention. What do you mean? How is the Bible different from any other book you've read? (You've probably read thousands.)
Curious,
Martina

***From:** Susy*
***To:** Martina*
***Sent:** Thursday, October 27*
***Subject:** Re: HOW is it different?*
Martina, the Bible is different because it's alive. It's not just words on a page. Each day before I began, I would pray and ask God to speak to me through the Bible. And he did! I found answers to a lot of my questions, and the more I read, the more I wanted to read. One day I read this verse about Jesus in Matthew 20: "The Son of Man did not come to be served, but to serve, and to give his life." I closed the Bible and my heart hurt as I realized that Jesus was everything that I was not. He was loving, giving, and unselfish. I wanted to be like that, too.
Love ya,
Susy

***From:** Martina*
***To:** Susy*
***Sent:** Thursday, October 27*
***Subject:** You ARE like that!*
You are like him, Susy. You make people feel like you really care. So how did it happen? How did you change? I'm not sure that it will work for me.
Confused,
Martina

***From:** Susy*
***To:** Martina*
***Sent:** Thursday, October 27*
***Subject:** It's not me . . .*
Martina, my life didn't change all at once. The more I read the Bible and got to know God, the more I wanted what he promises—an abundant life full of love, joy, and peace. So I asked him to help me, because I knew I couldn't have that on my own. I had tried before, and it hadn't worked. So I gave him my life with all of my weaknesses and mistakes and asked him to change me. It wasn't an overnight thing; it was just that, sin-by-sin, God replaced my desire to live for my own pleasure with the desire to please him. And that changed everything.
Love ya,
Susy

***From:** Martina*
***To:** Susy*
***Sent:** Friday, October 28*
***Subject:** Guess what?*
Susy, I'm going to try it. I bought a Bible last night. I just don't want to be empty anymore. I want what you have.
Much love,
Martina

When the door opens

When I wrote an e-mail *about* my friend Martina, and then accidentally sent it *to* Martina, a door suddenly opened and through it emerged a deep spiritual discussion with an unsaved friend. You can learn to recognize this crucial moment in a relationship. Suddenly a question or comment cuts through the surface chatter of everyday conversation and touches on the meaning of life, or who God is, or why evil exists. Those moments make you catch your breath as your heart beats a little harder. This is your chance to offer a piece of your story! Don't be afraid. Know that the Holy Spirit is at work and you are not alone in the moment. God is near.

Put one foot in front of the other

My family likes to spend time outside and we especially love to hike. When the kids were small, they ran and skipped with joy on the way out; but inevitably, they tuckered out on the return hike and dragged their boots, whining and complaining. To encourage them, we'd sing a goofy song from an animated Christmas TV special: *Put one foot in front of the other, and soon you'll be walking 'cross the floor. Just put one foot in front of the other, and soon you'll be walking out the door.* Somehow it always worked, and we would sing and march home.

Sharing your faith is much like those hikes with the kids: it can be hard and it can be discouraging. But you are not alone; many other Christians have passed this way. Be encouraged with some helpful ways to "just put one foot in front of the other."

Top ten tips for sharing your faith

1. Pray "God, use me." This is a prayer of yielding, telling God that you will do what he wants you to do. This is a prayer of faith, because you don't exactly know what you'll be doing, where you will be, or whom you will be talking to. This is also a prayer of Jesus: "Not my will, but yours" (Luke 22:42). This prayer will be answered, because God is constantly searching for those who want to join him in his work. And the best thing about this prayer? God is in control, so you can leave the results up to him.

2. Give people your full attention. This technique alone is so unusual that just practicing a "free attention giveaway"[27] will touch people. Jesus was so good at this. Often when approached, even when he was in a big crowd preaching or teaching, he would stop and take time for a face-to-face encounter. Jesus was never too busy to talk to someone who needed him. We can be like that, too. Here are some ways to give people your full attention:

- Stop what you're doing and turn to face the person directly.
- Use body language that signals openness. Uncross your arms, take off your sunglasses, nod and tilt your head as you listen.
- Smile and look into the person's eyes.
- Make small talk. Chat about the weather, kids, bills, the news. Notice what matters to the other person and remember for next time.
- Listen carefully to what is said, then follow up with, "What happened next?" or "How did you feel about that?"
- Say "Wow" when someone says something you find shocking or that you disagree strongly with.[28] "Wow" indicates surprise and interest instead of disagreement or disapproval.

3. Ask for permission to share. People are constantly bombarded with intrusive messages to buy so we've developed a simple survival mechanism: selective hearing. Without even consciously choosing, we control access to our attention like a volume knob. We turn up the volume when we're with a close friend, letting communication flow freely. With a new acquaintance or someone we don't quite trust, we turn the volume down, carefully monitoring how much we say and hear. For a stranger, especially one trying to sell us something? The volume goes off. We might be physically present but no communication takes place.

To turn up the volume control of communication we need permission, which is granted on the basis of trust and friendship. Canned presentations and forceful pronouncements are in danger of being completely tuned out. This is where relationships triumph. In a recent study, believers were asked "What or who was responsible for your coming to Christ?" Seventy-five to 90 percent cited a relationship with a friend or relative.[29] The purpose of permission in evangelism is to "create trust, get around the legal and social barriers to discussing your faith, and most importantly, to discern the leading of the Holy Spirit in someone's life."[30]

4. Share your story. At the beginning of this chapter, in the e-mail sent by mistake, I had the chance to share part of my story with my friend, Martina. Notice that I neither skipped over my mistakes nor provided every gory detail of my past. Instead I gave my friend a glimpse into my life before God and after God. Also, I tried to be authentic and honest, admitting that my life wasn't perfect the minute I began to follow Jesus. Instead, it was a sin-by-sin transformation.

Your own faith story works not only because it illustrates the change in your life, but also because it reassures people that they can experience that change as well. A young writer explains the power of story:

> We know that the Church won't miraculously cure us of our misery. What do you have left to persuade us? One thing: the story. We are story people. We know narratives, not ideas. Our surrogate parents were the TV and the VCR, and we can spew out entertainment trivia at the drop of a hat. We treat our ennui with stories, more and more stories, because they're the only things that make sense. . . . You wonder why we're so self-destructive, but we're looking for the one story with staying power, the destruction and redemption of our own lives. That's to your advantage: you have the best redemption story on the market.[31]

5. Unfold your experiences, even the painful ones. Like a wolf that creeps off to lick his wounds in the private darkness of his den, so do we hide our past wounds, mistakes, and regrets from our friends. But God can turn around our worst, most painful experiences and use them to help us reach out to others. Make yourself vulnerable.

Recently, God used a tragedy in Jan's life to open a door for her to share her faith. Jan explains:

> I think we should put into practice the holy boldness that God gives us. My nineteen-year-old son Joe, my darling, my baby, was murdered near our house in Florida. We live in an upper-class, really nice neighborhood. It was all over the news. . . . the shock of the community. Everyone wanted to know how I was doing. So I invited everyone in my neighborhood to lunch. The invitations read: 'Jan will share her faith and what helped her to overcome the tragedy of her son's murder.' People were curious. I gave my testimony and explained that the reason I have peace is because of the Lord, and that I am thankful to him for sustaining me through this agonizing experience. I used my tragedy to share God's love.

The result? Several women decided that day to follow Jesus.

6. Avoid churchy language. The object of sharing your faith is to find common ground with people you meet. Churchy or preachy language can frighten, intimidate, or even offend people who've had bad experiences with church or with Christians. It might surprise you that even the word *Christian* can shut down conversation and exploration by seekers. Why? The culture has changed. "Today, most nonbelievers were not brought up in the culture of the church and do not seek answers there. They don't share a common set of beliefs—they don't speak the language."[32] When sharing your faith, avoid words like *evangelism, seeker, kingdom, born again Christian, salvation, lost, personal savior*. Instead, like in the e-mail exchange, tell a part of your story that illustrates what God means to you, what you've learned from him, and how he works in your life. Since this is your story, use everyday language.

7. Keep it simple, but know when to go deeper. Read the Gospels to see how Jesus handled encounters with seekers. When people pulled him aside for one-on-one time, Jesus didn't preach a three-point sermon or tell the complete story of his life. He didn't close with the sinner's prayer or have the person fill out a questionnaire. Instead, Jesus commonly responded in one of three ways:

- *With a simple question:*
  "Who do you say I am?" (Mark 8:29) or "Do you want to get well?" (John 5:6).
- *With a short observation:*
  "I tell you the truth, no one can see the kingdom of God unless he is born again" (John 3:3).
- *With forgiveness or healing of a desperate need:*
  "Go . . . your faith has healed you" (Mark 10:52).

In my e-mail conversation with Martina, I related my faith story in steps, waiting for a question or positive response before going deeper.

8. Cultivate humility. Becoming humble sounds simple, but it is probably the most challenging item on this list. Benjamin Franklin, one of America's founding fathers as well as an inventor, millionaire, and all-around genius, confessed that pride was the most difficult virtue to master. He worked very hard to eliminate pride from his life, but just when he thought he had done it, he found himself being proud of his accomplishment.

The Bible illustrates clearly the problem of pride and its bitter consequences. The Jews were judged for their pride, and the wicked cities of Sodom and Gomorrah were characterized by pride. Lucifer rebelled out of pride and a desire to dethrone God. Jesus taught that the proud will be humbled, but the humble will be lifted up (Matt. 23:12).

The easiest, and perhaps only, way to achieve humility is through denying self and serving others. Paul put it this way: "Though I am free and belong to no man, I make myself a slave to everyone, to win as many as possible" (1 Cor. 9:19). Serving others can be as simple as opening a door for someone at the bank or as complicated and costly as adopting a Romanian orphan. God's call is for you to forget yourself, take up your cross, and serve. The first step: forget self.

9. Recognize your uniqueness. Whatever your particular personality or talents, God can use you to touch other people. He did with Randy: "I always felt different. I am extremely relationally wired—much more so than the average male. I invest a lot of emotion in relationships." When he was in his twenties, Randy served for several years as a missionary to China and discovered there that "relationships with friends are a very important part of culture in Asia." Since then, he's served as a pastor in a Chinese church, worked for a missions agency leading trips to China, and befriended many Chinese nationals working or studying here in the United States. What made him feel awkward when he was younger has proved to be a great asset in sharing his faith with Chinese friends. God will use your uniqueness: there is no such thing as "one size fits all" evangelism.[33]

10. Leave the outcome to God. When the door opens to share your faith with a friend, perhaps using *The Da Vinci Code,* grab the opportunity. Talk, serve, lead, teach, give, help, confront, witness—whatever you are called to do at that crucial moment, do with all your heart. Then, release the results to God because even though you have obediently shared your faith, your friend might not make a decision to follow Jesus for many years. But your part is crucial, because each Christian who encounters a non-Christian is like a link in a chain. "It's great to be the last link in the chain," says Bill Kraftson of Search Ministries, "but it's not more important than any other link. We just need to make sure we're not the missing link."[34] So relax, know that you are responsible for just one link, and that it's God who forges the links into a chain that stretches to eternity.

God, Use Me!

No painful or difficult experience need go to waste. If you let him, God will use your emotional and spiritual wounds to draw you closer to himself and to others. Use a journal to detail a painful life experience. Next, pray that God will take the experience and use it to accomplish his purposes in the lives of people. Last, tear out the page as you thank God that he makes all things new.[35]

CHAPTER
FIVE

The Strategy

Taking The Da Vinci Code *dare.*

"I am not ashamed of the gospel."

—ROMANS 1:16

BOOK CLUB members are known for their passion for books, which often results in intense discussions. Tempers can flare when a controversial book like *The Da Vinci Code* is chosen. Although the following account is fictional, it reflects common reactions to *The Da Vinci Code.*

Hayward Book Club News, October 2005

Report on the September Meeting by Nicole Palmer

Tempers flared last month as the Hayward Book Club gathered to discuss the popular thriller *The Da Vinci Code.* "I don't know if I'm ever coming back," said Mrs. K., a longtime member, as she left the room. "They were yelling and pounding on their chairs! I told them, 'People, it's just a book. Nothing to get excited about.' But they wouldn't listen."

The controversy began when the book was initially chosen as the September selection. Several members refused to read it or attend the book club meeting. "*The Da Vinci Code* is a dangerous book," wrote Mrs. R., in a letter mailed to the club secretary. "It should be burned."

A week before the scheduled meeting, Ms. B. wrote a letter to the editor of the *Hayward Daily News.*

> Dear Editor:
>
> Dan Brown is a dangerous goddess worshipper who seeks to persuade the naïve to his twisted point of view. I urge all of you in the community to protest with me against this piece of trash masquerading as a best-selling novel. Please join me September 14 for a protest march outside the Hayward Book Club, whose members have chosen to read this vile book.
>
> Sincerely, Ms. B.

Hayward Book Club members braved a dozen protesters waving signs that read "Da Vinci Code Deceives" and "We Frown on Dan Brown." Inside, after closing the windows and locking the door, members pulled copies of *The Da Vinci Code* from under coats and out of bags and got down to business.

What happened behind closed doors? Ms. G. explained: "Everyone seemed a little nervous, but before long the room was buzzing as we tried to figure out the plot. We got into a long discussion about whether Mona Lisa was really Leonardo da Vinci in drag. Then someone brought up that thing about Jesus being married.

"We argued back and forth, a few people turning red in the face, until finally someone pointed out that Jesus had no house, no money, no donkey. What woman would want to marry an itinerant teacher with nowhere to lay his head? Running around the desert, hanging out with fishermen, always surrounded by big groups of people—he had no time for a wife. We decided he had bigger things on his mind."

Heads nodded, settling the matter. Next, the book club took a break for coffee and pumpkin pie. And that's when it happened.

One member (no one's quite sure who) said that *The Da Vinci Code* was the dumbest book he'd ever read, and he couldn't believe that it was now the best-selling novel of all time. "People are so ignorant," he allegedly said. Responses from the group included a chaotic mix of declarations such as "I loved the book," and "I couldn't put it down," with the coffee break rapidly turning into a group argument, and then a shouting match accompanied by red faces and pointing fingers.

With the Hayward Book Club hastily adjourning for the night, Mrs. M. expressed regret. "It's just too bad we didn't get to finish our meeting. This book confused me and I never really figured out what the 'Code' is? Do you know?"

I had to admit, I didn't.

Next month's book selection: *The Eight Essential Steps to Conflict Resolution* by Dudley Weeks.

The Da Vinci Code: Love it or hate it?

Reactions to *The Da Vinci Code* range along a broad spectrum from loathing to rapture. Audience reactions to books and movies are very unpredictable, a frustrating fact for publishers and film studios, who would love to develop a surefire system to predict which projects will be blockbuster hits and which will not even recover production costs. But so far such a system has yet to be invented.

What makes a book like *The Da Vinci Code* grab hold of the hearts and minds of readers and climb the best-seller lists? No one knows. Even writers who have once produced a best seller often fail to repeat. The odds are against it. In the year 2004, a record 195,000 new books were released in the United States. Of those books, less than 1 percent made the best-seller list.[36] Publishers would love to know how to transform the other 99 percent into best sellers.

Have you ever loved a book and passed it on to a good friend who hated it? It happens all the time. And it's the same, of course, with *The Da Vinci Code.* Except that in the case of this novel, millions have loved it. Chances are you know some of those fans. Don't make the same mistake as the very opinionated members of the Hayward Book Club and get into shouting matches over the merits of the book because you'll never get the chance to delve into what really matters: the obstacles that keep a person from choosing to follow Jesus.

Again, take note of the accounts of Jesus' interactions; rather than violent arguments or angry debates, he conducted quiet conversations, always taking a keen interest in the condition of the heart.

While so far this book has introduced the idea of using *The Da Vinci Code* to share your faith and has provided some general tips on evangelism, we turn now to specific examples of encounters, questions, and topics you're likely to hear, and creative ways to respond to those questions and turn them into productive discussions. But first, we want to pass along a few guidelines to consider as you use *The Da Vinci Code* to share your faith.

Da Vinci Code faith-sharing strategies

1. Acknowledge the entertainment value of *The Da Vinci Code.* When you're talking to someone who loved the story, don't immediately rattle off a list of the historical errors or detail the theological issues because you'll shut down any potential discussion by offending fans. It's disrespectful to their tastes not to acknowledge that many people have enjoyed reading the book, even if you haven't. Why not just agree that the book is entertaining? You might be appalled by what you perceive as an attack on the faith, but millions enjoyed the roller-coaster ride of suspense and intrigue. Perhaps they liked the puzzles, the Leonardo da Vinci subplot, or the European setting. If you want to get beyond a surface discussion, beware of making a hasty denouncement.

2. Know that not everyone cares. Don't assume that every reader has keyed into the controversial subjects of the book. After all, not everyone is interested in spiritual matters. You can determine the level of interest with a few well-placed questions, such as "Do you think the book is true?" or "Was there anything in the book that surprised or shocked you?" If someone is only interested in discussing the Louvre and seeing the *Mona Lisa* on a recent visit, your discussion may never go beneath the surface.

3. Avoid preachiness. Aim for a discussion with give and take between both parties so you can figure out what the other person is thinking and feeling. If you take over the discussion and begin to tell a *Da Vinci Code* fan what's wrong with the book, you will quickly be tuned out. When someone falls in love with a book or a film, they become emotionally engaged and are not easily dissuaded by facts, logic, or historical proof. Therein lies the power of story; *The Da Vinci Code* bypasses the facts and aims for the heart, where it sticks. Even when presented with the facts, many people continue to believe the claims of the book. Why? Because love is not logical. People buy into the claims of the book and it becomes part of them. Avoid preachiness because you'll offend them; you could be attacking something they love.

4. Read a debunker book or two. Several great books and videos examine *The Da Vinci Code*'s claims, item by item, and disprove them with facts. Scholars agree that the history in the novel is faulty, and plenty of people have the credentials and resources to highlight Dan Brown's errors. Read a debunker to give you confidence. You probably won't be able to answer every future question or point of discussion, but you'll be familiar with the issues and able to direct the curious to helpful resources. (In the back of this book, you'll find a list of resources.)

5. Carry a cheat sheet. If you know you'll be talking to someone about *The Da Vinci Code*, or maybe even about a particular topic, create a "cheat sheet" that lists some of the main points you want to make. Perhaps a list of eight reasons Jesus wasn't married (from chapter 6). Politicians call these lists "talking points" and study them before interviews. Carry your cheat sheet with you and review it just before your discussion. If you feel led, you might want to pull it out to show the person you're talking to. Once, when talking to a friend, I used a cheat sheet with some verses written on it. She noticed, asked for a closer look, and then took it home.

6. Return question for question. Rather than answer and risk ending the discussion, ask a question and see if you can take the discussion deeper. If someone asks you if you think the Bible is true, answer back with "What do you think?" The answer may surprise you and spark a richer line of discussion.

7. Avoid rabbit trails. Sometimes people want to chat about side issues such as the secret organizations in the book or whether Tom Hanks is the right actor to play Langdon in the movie. That's okay at first, but try to head the discussion into deeper waters at some point. You will need the Holy Spirit's help. Pray and ask God to guide you as you endeavor to steer the discussion to more serious matters.

8. Make plans to talk further. Ending a conversation can be much harder than starting one. Here are some possible conversation-ending strategies for when you've had a *Da Vinci Code* encounter:

- Plan for both of you to read a debunker and then get together to discuss it. (See appendix C, "For Further Reading . . .")
- When you don't know how to answer a question, promise to find the answer for a future meeting.
- Make plans to see the movie together and go out for pizza afterward to talk.
- Meet together to work through *The Da Vinci Code* issues using the Bible.
- Together attend a local Bible study aimed at people who are investigating the gospel.

- If they ask questions you cannot answer, direct them to your pastor.
- Say good-bye and pray silently for them as they leave.

Read on, as we share some more *Da Vinci Code* moments. These encounters ranged from five minutes to several hours to much longer relationships. We'll share effective ways to answer some of the questions raised in the book and demonstrate how to move the discussion along as the Spirit allows.

The goal as you cultivate *Da Vinci Code* faith encounters is always to delve deeper into spiritual things. "Our immediate goal with people is not to lead them to Jesus, but consistently to take the initiative to join them in the places where God is working in their lives and to help them take the next step in their journeys toward faith . . . we look for opportunities to plant the seeds of biblical truth."[37]

Once, when Jesus encountered some curious fishermen who later became his disciples, he directed them to go deeper, where the fishing was best: "Put out into deep water" (Luke 5:4). *The Da Vinci Code* offers a unique opportunity for you to follow Jesus to where the fishing is best. Don't be afraid, for there is nothing more exciting than to be present when God is working in someone's life. Put out into deep water; you don't want to miss it.

Put Out into Deep Water

Pick up your Bible and read the book of Luke. Every time Jesus talks to or touches a person, use a pen and make a tiny star at the spot. When you're finished, page back through Luke and notice how many people Jesus encountered face-to-face. Jesus is still at work today in the lives of people around you. He is still fishing; let's get in the boat.

CHAPTER

SIX

The Five-Minute Chat

Was Jesus married?

"It is the Father, living in me, who is doing his work."

—JOHN 14:10

THE SUBWAY bounced crazily. The woman standing behind my seat stumbled forward and grabbed for a handhold.

Instinctively, I reached out to steady her.

Fear etched her forehead. She clutched her purse to her chest. Her eyes glinted a warning as they shot a look at me.

I smiled. "Quite a ride today, huh?"

She ignored me.

"I can't believe the crowd. Is it like this every day?"

Her tension thawed slightly. "Today's worse than usual."

I watched her eyes. They caught on my *Da Vinci Code* book cover. I lifted the book an inch from my lap and searched for her response. "Have you read this yet?"

I barely heard her breathe, "Great book!"

I chose my adjective carefully, "It's unique."

She nodded and turned her shoulders slightly toward me.

Give her space, I thought. I yawned and stretched my legs forward. "What did you like about it?"

"It's answered a lot of questions I've had about the Bible. I'm really glad I read it!"

". . . Jesus as a married man makes infinitely more sense than our standard biblical view of Jesus as a bachelor."

"Why?" Sophie asked.

"Because Jesus was a Jew," Langdon said, taking over while Teabing searched for his book, "and the social decorum during that time virtually forbid a Jewish man to be unmarried. According to Jewish custom, celibacy was condemned, and the obligation for a Jewish father was to find a suitable wife for his son. If Jesus were not married, at least one of the Bible's gospels would have mentioned it and offered some explanation for His unnatural state of bachelorhood."

—*The Da Vinci Code*, p. 245

I grinned. She couldn't be serious, could she? But I held my voice steady. "Like what questions?"

"I've always wondered whether Jesus was married or not. Now I know he was!"

"What convinced you?"

"Well . . ." The tip of her tongue slowly traced her lower lip as she stared at the handgrip. "I guess it all makes sense." She looked directly at me.

I gave her a safe nod.

"Jesus loved Mary Magdalene. And it was the custom for parents to arrange their kids' marriages when they were young. Anyway, the

Bible doesn't say anywhere that he wasn't married, does it? Do you know?"

This woman was searching for an answer. She had opened the door. She was confused about a lot of things, but I had possibly only thirty seconds to help her. It might be five minutes between stops—so, at best, three hundred seconds! I prayed quickly. "God what should I say?"

At that moment, I couldn't remember anything I had studied. Only one statement that someone else had made recently came to me. I borrowed it. "The Bible says that after Jesus rises from the dead, he appears to Mary in the garden. When she sees him, she thinks he's the gardener. 'Mary,' he says in a way only Jesus could speak. Then she recognizes him and cries out, 'Rabboni,' which means 'Teacher!' Imagine—not 'Honey,' not 'my dear,' but 'Dr. Teacher!' "

The woman grinned.

"And then, to top that off, he doesn't hug her. He doesn't tell her he's missed her. Instead he orders her to let go of his feet and commands her to go tell the disciples what she's seen. Not a real intimate relationship!"

"If my husband did that, I'd kill him!" We laughed.

Her next words were swallowed up by "Lake Merritt Station. Exit on the right!"

"Excuse me?"

"That Bible verse, where is it?" The door beeped open and she was out.

"Book of John, I think. Somewhere near the end," and the door closed. I lifted my hand as the train rumbled past her. She smiled back.

I began to feel guilty. I'd really messed up my chance to share Jesus with someone. I should have had a better answer. I didn't even know where that verse was! I beat myself up the rest of the way to my stop. Can a five-minute meeting be worth anything to God?

Later, when I was praying, the answers came.

Quick Encounters

- *How much time did Jesus' encounter with the woman at the well take?* Jesus asked for a drink. The woman basically gave him a rejection. He looked into her, loved her anyway, and offered her water that would take away all her thirsts. She dashed away believing she had seen the Messiah (John 4:7–29).
- *How long did the argument take to convince Nathanael that Jesus was the Son of God?* Philip told his friend he had found the promised Messiah. Nathanael, the better scholar, argued against Philip's reasoning. Nathanael followed Philip anyway. Then Nathaniel looked for himself and believed Jesus was the Son of God (John 1:45).
- *How hard was it for Philip to convince the Ethiopian to believe?* Philip was on the road. God set up the scene. The Ethiopian reader asked about what he read. Philip gave him a sensible answer. The Ethiopian wanted to be baptized right then (Acts 8:26–38).
- Again and again God takes a short-term situation and turns those few seconds into a new life of eternity! It's not the work that we do; it's his Spirit that convinces a person.

God can work with any time or effort that I'll give him. He chooses to use my mouth, my situation, my minutes. I need to let him take control. He'll work on the hearer's heart. Even Jesus got out of the way so the Father could work through him. He put it this way when his own disciple had a lapse of belief: "Don't you believe that I am in the Father, and that the Father is in me? The words I say to you are not just my own. Rather, it is the Father, living in me, who is doing his work" (John 14:10).

Was Jesus married?

The Da Vinci Code raises intriguing questions. I'm surprised at the number of people who ask me, "Could Jesus have been married?" Eight biblical reasons are strong evidences that Jesus wasn't married:

1. The Bible doesn't mention Jesus' wife. The Bible doesn't say that Jesus wasn't married, but it doesn't say he was, either. His wife should have been mentioned somewhere in the gospels.

2. Jesus never spoke about his wife. If she existed, wouldn't he have shown partiality to her out of respect for her position? In his daily life, wouldn't he have spent time apart with her? Particularly noteworthy, at the crucifixion, Jesus doesn't refer to a wife. If you were dying early in your married life, wouldn't one of your greatest concerns be for your wife or your child's welfare? Instead, Jesus' one pressing concern is for his mother. In one of his last breaths, he asks one of his special disciples, John, to take his mother in (John 19:27). That would have been Jesus' wife's responsibility. Family takes care of family (1 Tim. 5:8).

3. No one tries to contact Jesus through his wife. At the wedding of Cana (John 2:1–10), it's his mother who is the contact point, not his wife. There is never any interaction between Jesus' wife and any other women mentioned in the Bible. By not mentioning her, we can assume she does not exist.

4. Other godly men were celibate. It was rare for a man not to be married in Bible times. Although being married was the tradition, some men, particularly rabbis, were granted the right to be celibate. Other godly men in the Bible didn't have sexual relationships. In the Old Testament, Jeremiah, one of the great prophets, was single. John the Baptist was unmarried. Most scholars believe that Paul was also single. A whole group of religious Jews called Essenes practiced celibacy. These men lived in Qumran, Israel and left the Dead Sea Scrolls behind.

Jesus also talked about men who chose to be celibate or eunuchs so they could serve God completely and not have the concerns of marriage (Matt. 19:10–12). Although Jesus didn't claim to live this godly way, he was humble and didn't boast of his righteousness. He did, however, say his goal in life was to give glory to God, to serve him completely (Matt. 26:39; John 6:38). Would Jesus choose a lifestyle that could possibly distract him from the goal that God gave him?

5. Jesus didn't act married. He selected twelve men with whom he did practically everything—traveled, ministered, prayed, ate, and camped out. Then there were the three special ones—Peter, James, and John. He took them to the mountain to see his glory, his transfiguration (Mark 9:2). No women accompanied them. Wouldn't a wife be invited along to know his true identity?

6. The apostle Paul didn't use him as an example of a married man. Some time after Christ's resurrection a debate apparently arose as to whether Christians were permitted to marry. On the side of permitting Christians to marry, Paul says in 1 Corinthians 7, "since there is so much immorality, each man should have his own wife, and each woman her own husband . . . if they cannot control themselves, they should marry, for it is better to marry than to burn with passion" (1 Cor. 7:2, 9). Paul continues, "I would like you to be free from concern. An unmarried man is concerned about the Lord's affairs—how he can please the Lord. But a married man is concerned about the affairs of this world—how he can please his wife—his interests are divided" (1 Cor. 7:32–34). He uses as evidence certain men who had taken their wives along in their missionary endeavors: the apostles, Peter, and Jesus' own brothers (1 Cor. 9:5). If indeed Christ were married, wouldn't Paul have mentioned the Lord Jesus himself in his list of those who took wives along in ministry? This question alone seems to silence the discussion.

7. If Jesus were married, why wouldn't the soldiers have captured him at home rather than in an open garden upon the deception of Judas? Instead, in Luke 9:58–62, Jesus says, "Foxes have holes and birds of the air have nests, but the Son of Man has no place to lay his head." In other words, he had no residence. He said to another man, "Follow me." Another said, "I will follow you, Lord; but first let me go back and say good-bye to my family." Jesus replied, "No one who puts his hand to the plow and looks back is fit for service in the kingdom of God." So, for a disciple, service to God comes first. The Bible says about family life, "If anyone does not provide for his relatives, and especially for his immediate family, he has denied the faith and is worse than an unbeliever" (1 Tim. 5:8). Jesus surely would not be homeless and drag a wife around with "no place to lay her head," too. The marriage would be one of inconvenience, at best.

8. Jesus' main goal on earth was to die as the just payment for all men's sins. Jesus explained that he was going to die on the cross, and it was the sacrifice that had to be made for sins (Matt. 26:26–28). He and others knew this from the beginning of his ministry (John 1:29). This would not be a wholesome match for any woman nor family.

Novelist Dan Brown adds a son and daughter to Jesus' family line. God's Son as a dad would certainly have brought many teachable moments as Jesus fathered his little ones and taught the necessary lessons of love, training, and discipline. Those aren't in the Bible, either.

In *The Da Vinci Code*, Sophie rediscovers her brother many years after Jesus' life on earth. They are distant descendants of Jesus. Ridiculous complications would follow from Jesus' grandchildren and great-great-grandchildren. What kind of people would these progeny be? Partial gods? The numbers of these children today, two thousand years after the fact, would possibly be in the millions. Would they still be considered a sacred family? In this world of divorce, wedlock, half brothers and sisters, stepchildren, adopted children, and intermarriage with people who are not gods, an accurate genealogy of Jesus' true descendants would be impossible. And if you couldn't trace your bloodline to him, you'd be a nobody. There would be so many people related somehow to Jesus, it would be of little importance.

I'm thankful that God treats all of us who have faith in Jesus the same way. We are his own first-generation children, adopted into his family (Rom. 8:23). As his kids, God loves us, disciplines us, and helps us to grow (Heb. 12:5–11). This fact alone gives ordinary people hope. We can all be part of Jesus' family!

Often we have only a few minutes—or even seconds—to share a sound bite of lasting hope. God may give you that chance to bring his message. *The Da Vinci Code*'s claim of Jesus' marriage is a great starting place, but preparation is essential.

CHAPTER
SEVEN

The Art Lesson

Is the Mona Lisa *really a man?*

"The Lord is . . . not wanting anyone to perish,
but everyone to come to repentance."

—2 PETER 3:9

KIDS, WHAT DO you think of *this* portrait?"

Mona Lisa stared at them from the poster. I had invited a group of eight- to twelve-year-old children and their parents over because I was concerned about the backwash of *The Da Vinci Code* book and movie on our kids. The three parents grinned knowingly at one another. The five kids said nothing.

I tried to start the conversation. "It was painted in the early 1500s, during the High Renaissance in Italy."

"You mean it's famous?" asked Luke with eyes wide.

"Very famous! And old."

The kids looked at each other, some shaking their heads.

"What do you think, Luke?"

"She's okay, I guess, but I'm glad we don't have her hanging in our living room."

Kara leaned in a little closer. "I think it's kind of pretty. The colors are nice."

"I bet she's standing in front of one of those fake scenes at the photographer's. That one looks like something from *Peter Pan*." Michael looked around for his audience's encouragement.

I looked past him at Dennea. She was staring right into *Mona Lisa*'s eyes. "What do you imagine the model's personality is like?"

"She looks like maybe a normal person of that time. She doesn't have real fancy clothes, no velvet, no jewels, no crown. But she's dressed nice with that little net thing over her hair." Dennea played with her earring.

"Look how soft her hands look," agreed Kara.

"She doesn't look like she's much fun." Michael screwed up his face into a fake *Mona Lisa* pose.

Kara sat up straight, a little *Mona Lisa* grin testing her lips. She shook her head. "You just try sitting for hours while somebody paints you, Michael. She can't be having a great time! At least she tried smiling. But it looks like she got tired of holding her mouth that way."

Dennea smiled and nodded at her best friend, Kara, then picked up a cookie and took a tiny bite. Michael mocked her, pursing his lips, faking little kisses at the imaginary cookie he held in front of his mouth. Dennea blushed while Kara looked at him cross-eyed, stuck out her tongue, and rolled her eyes to the ceiling.

What's androgyny?

Kids! That's how the art lesson started. I had chosen to couch my lesson in a summer drawing activity. "That little smile is why some people say the model has charm."

"Hey, where are her eyebrows?" Giggles all around.

"Women of that day plucked them out or even shaved them. Styles change. As girls, we plucked out all our eyebrows and then drew new ones in with an eyebrow pencil in an exact shape that we thought was beautiful. I even had a stencil." That mother seemed to be really getting into it.

Some of the kids groaned; the boys laughed. Daniel pretended to paint eyebrows on Luke, who threw a fake punch to his jaw. His mother frowned and Luke moved to the other side of the circle.

"Do you think the model is pretty?"

"Not pretty, but not ugly either."

"She just looks normal—but not someone you'd look at and say, 'Wow!' about."

"Hey, try this." Luke moved his head back and forth staring at the painting from one position and then the other. "Her eyes keep watching you!" Several of the other kids moved around to see if he was right. "Cool!"

"That must be why it's famous, right Mrs. Monroe?"

"Actually there are different opinions of why she's famous. Some people like how deep the paint and varnish are. There are maybe fifty coats on the entire panel. These seem to make the painting glow from life and light within."

"Maybe the thickness could be a sign of something else. Maybe the artist wasn't satisfied with the painting and kept redoing it. I painted a portrait of Luke's grandpa like that. I started it years ago. I can't throw it away—I need to finish it, but I just keep trying to redo it over the old one, again and again, hoping to get the wrong parts right. Then I revarnished it and hung it up. From there I see I've missed the target again. It's never stayed on a wall for more than half a day!" Dennea's mother looked in her lap and shook her head sadly.

"Dan Brown, the author of *The Da Vinci Code*, thinks the painting is important for another reason. He says it shows *androgyny*."[38] I had read the book carefully. Dan Brown majored on this point to prove some of his cultish thoughts. I feared this lie could easily lead young minds away from the truths of God.

"What's that word mean?"

"*Androgynous* is a term that people usually use for flowers. It means they have both male and female parts, a stamen and a pistil." The kids looked confused.

"How many of you think this painting is of a woman?"

All hands went up.

"Whatever da Vinci was up to, his *Mona Lisa* is neither male nor female according to *The Da Vinci Code*," a parent clarified.

"Nuh uh," someone groaned.

"That's dumb. It's a girl. Look at her dress. If Luke put it on, he wouldn't look that good."

"Shut up!" Luke countered.

"But what about her nose? It does look kind of like a man's nose, doesn't it?"

"I think it looks Italian. Didn't you say she was Italian?"

"Actually she *was* Italian. This is a painting of a real woman, twenty-four-year-old Madonna Lisa di Gioconda, which translates, *Lisa from Gioconda*." Some of the kids' faces were blank. "You know like Leonardo da Vinci, which means Leonardo *from the area of Vinci*. Some people call him da Vinci rather than his given name, Leonardo. So back to Madonna Lisa di Gioconda; some people call the painting *La Gioconda* from the name of her neighborhood. This painting is supposedly an exact copy of her looks."

Da Vinci in drag?

"Mrs. Monroe, doesn't one of *The Da Vinci Code* characters say it might be a self-portrait of Leonardo da Vinci, dressed up to look like a woman?"[39]

"Yuck!"

Giggles again.

I showed them a transparency of Leonardo's self-portrait—reversed and resized—and then slid the film of *Mona Lisa* over the top. "Check this out. Do you think *Mona Lisa* could be Leonardo cross-dressing?"

Kara was really concentrating. "Look at the forehead. His is much lumpier."

"Her cheekbones are stronger. The skin underneath her cheeks is caved in," Michael added.

"*Mona Lisa*'s chin is much smaller."

"Her lips are way different."

"It's not the same person, if that's what you mean." Daniel's voice was strong and sure.

"That's exactly what I'm asking. Typically men and women's faces differ not only in facial structure, but also in design. Let's see what makes up the human face. Take your paper and your pencil, and let's get started. We start with an oval. Next we'll divide it in half. Now divide the bottom section into thirds. The top line . . ."

From there, I taught the students to draw a blank face—one that was just a generic start to a portrait.

I had hoped that along with the art lesson I could perhaps provide some insight into God's Word, contrasting its thoughts with those of *The Da Vinci Code.* After the book, and now the movie, Dan Brown's antibiblical views have even confused some children.

You are unique

Most of the artists had finished the blank face. "This is the basic shape of a human head. But look at the person across the table from you and then at your drawing. They're not the same, are they? If you are drawing a female face, the oval will normally be thinner; the jaw line will be narrower and shorter; and the nose will be shorter and probably thinned on the bridge." I demonstrated these changes as I sketched.

I noticed some were beginning to change their blanks. "Just watch for a second, and then you can get going on your own drawing. I have copies of the blanks I've drawn for each of you, so you can go back to the beginning some other time."

I began illustrating on another blank that I had drawn ahead of time. "If you are drawing a male, the brow line will be heavier and probably widened a bit. The ears will probably be larger, the nose wider, heavier and longer (especially on an adult), and the jaw longer, wider, and more emphasized. Now here's the female. From these two blanks, it's easy to see the difference between male and female faces. Even before any of the details are added, the shape will already have shown the sex of the study. God made a perfect pattern for each one—male and female. Then he made each person different from the others, absolutely unique!"

"Do you know that the Bible says that God knew what you were going to look like even when you were in your mother's womb? Psalm 139 says 'he knit you together.' "

"Let's look at the *Mona Lisa* again. Does she have a male or female structure?"

"Her chin and jaw are too little for a man."

"Her lips are thin. A man would look sissy with those lips."

"What's wrong with her nose? Why is it so long and bumpy?"

"Mrs. Monroe said she was Italian. That's an Italian nose!"

"Well, if men have bigger foreheads and wilder eyebrows, there's no doubt she's a girl!"

"I think you're all right. *Mona Lisa* is feminine. She is not a combination of a man and a woman—in other words, no androgyny there."

"Well, are you ready to try sketching a face yourself? We'll use the person's face straight across from you at the table. You'll have to take turns."

"Start with a blank, then draw the special differences that your model has—male or female. Then because each person's face is unique, you'll have to look very carefully at his or her features. Don't just draw what you think should be there. Try to make the changes in the blank according to what you see." I showed them how to measure what they saw with a pencil. "The first artists will have the next twenty minutes to draw their models."

Androgyny

The artists were instantly busy, measuring by one closed eye and a raised pencil. The youngest children, of course, were finished much earlier than the others. They went outside to play with the dog as soon as they were done or had lost interest.

I hoped each would not only learn to sketch a face, but also that they might understand something new about God.

Leonardo da Vinci's *Mona Lisa* supposedly has a hidden message: in order to be enlightened, the soul must have balance between male and female elements.[40] The Egyptian god, Amon, and the Egyptian goddess of fertility, Isis, combine together—aMonIsis, Amon' Isis, or Amon L'isa—to finally form the words, *Mona Lisa.*[41] She is supposedly the embodiment of the androgynous union of male and female, "Da Vinci's little secret, the reason for *Mona Lisa*'s knowing smile."[42]

Later, Dan Brown extends this lie to supposedly show that Jesus Christ needed to have a wife in order to be complete.

I thought this drawing lesson could possibly be a good lead-in for a parent and child to discuss the fact that we are not gods, nor are we missing just one essential element to be a god—*The Da Vinci Code*'s claim that we need sexual union with another person!

At the end of the first twenty minutes, I stopped the group. "How about changing jobs? Models are now artists." The new artists began their turn.

On the other hand, these kids were pretty young. But soon they would be in those developing years when they feel so terribly insecure. What they really needed more than anything was just to know that God made them, loved them, and wanted each of them to be unique and complete in his love.

I could see the artists would soon be finished. I called the younger ones back in. They collapsed into their seats laughing and smelling of the fresh air and soil. I spoke over the crowns of the artists' heads.

"Isn't it amazing how Jesus, the Creator, designed the human face, the human body, you? He gave each one of you here everything you need to be a complete adult. Your ears hear. And your brain takes what you hear, and you analyze the instructions and put it into working plans that you can use to make a drawing. Your eyes see. You understand what's in front of you, and you flatten it out in your thinking. Then you make comparisons between what you see and what you draw."

God thinks you are worthwhile

"Some of you are probably pretty happy with what you drew. Others think you'll never be artists. But God has made you each unique. Your own face is not like anyone else's. Your thoughts and abilities are different, too. Most of us think there are parts of us we'd like to exchange, but according to God, he loves you just the way you are. Not one of you is better than the others. You're different, and that's by design." I picked up my Bible to read. "Psalm 139 says:

> You have searched me and you know me.
> You know when I sit and when I rise; you perceive my thoughts
> from afar.
> You discern my going out and my lying down; you are familiar
> with all my ways.
> Before a word is on my tongue you know it completely, O Lord . . .
> All the days ordained for me were written in your book
> before one of them came to be.
> How precious to me are your thoughts, O God!
> How vast is the sum of them!
> Were I to count them, they would outnumber the grains of sand
> (Psalm 139:1–4, 16–18)."

"God knows you completely and still loves you. He thinks you are worthwhile and wants to have a relationship with you today and forever."

"Okay. Let's get back in our drawing teams. Show your partner how they look to you."

The kids laughed, groaned, complained, and complimented each other.

"This is a skill you'll have to work on. You can each learn to draw a better likeness, and the more you practice, the better you'll get. But you'll never be perfect. Even skilled artists have a hard time getting a good likeness. Now, since you know how to draw a face, which of you thinks you could draw a picture of God?"

Michael, of course, raised his hand.

"Michael, how could you know what God looks like? The Bible says God's a spirit and spirits don't have flesh and bones." Kara grinned at Dennea and the other kids in victory.

"When I get through drawing him, then you'll know what he looks like, too!"

Everybody laughed.

Michael thought better of his answer and corrected himself, "Okay, I guess I couldn't draw God."

"Look at your drawing. Do you think if you tried again and got a really expert likeness of your friend across the table that anyone could really know the person you drew?"

"What do you mean? Could someone recognize them?"

"No. Could they know what that person is like? Could they know the model's personality?"

"Nobody can draw that good! Even if you take a photograph, you can't see into a person's heart," Kara softly stated.

"And it takes years to really *know* a person. You have to go through different things with them to see how they act; you have to be with somebody a lot to have a relationship with them," Dennea added, smiling at Kara.

"Some of you know the Lord; you have a relationship with him. What do you know about him and how do you know it?"

Daniel partially raised his hand, then put it back down quickly.

"Do you want to say something, Daniel?"

"Well. I was just thinking that we know that the Lord is strong."

"Good. How do you know that?"

"Well, if you go to Yosemite, you can know that. Just look at the huge cliffs, the rocks, the canyons and you know someone strong made it."

"Good, Daniel. I agree. Does anyone else know the Lord well enough to name one of his characteristics?"

"I know he loves me." Kara looked around for approval. Of course, Dennea nodded immediately.

"So, how do you know that?"

"Because the Bible says so. Those verses in Psalms 139 that you just read show that."

Dennea raised her hand. "And we know he cares about knowing us and having a relationship with us from what those verses say."

"Right. And from that, then, we can know that the Lord is loving and kind. He knows and abides by justice. Once the Lord has made a law, he keeps it. He is righteous and good. He also tells us that in his Word," one of the parents added.

The Da Vinci Code god or the true God?

"Through *The Da Vinci Code*, Dan Brown's characters show a different Lord—an incomplete, untrue picture of him. They say one part of God is male—like a man. And he needs a female part, a goddess, to be complete. Worship of this supposed female part of god (the goddess of fertility) goes clear back to the Egyptians. And so does worship of the male part of god (the god of fertility, Amon). They claim that because this worship was done in the past, it must be true and we need to worship like that today. The characters of *The Da Vinci Code* say that the Lord is a god of nature. These story characters insist that there are people who worship Mother Earth today and the characters know they are right."[43]

"But these made-up characters are wrong. The Lord our God is one. Jesus is God as the Bible shows him over and over. The Bible is not a fictional story like *The Da Vinci Code* is."

"According to the Bible, you can know God yourself. In fact, God wants to be your Father who will never stop loving you, never leave you. He will never die. The Bible says in John 1:12, 13 that 'to all who received him, to those who believed in his name, he gave the right to become children of God—children born not of natural descent, nor of human decision or a husband's will, but born of God.' "

"If you want to know more about this, just come talk to me or Dennea's mother. We can help you to have a relationship with God."

The art lesson ended. Oh, except for an encouragement for each of them to practice drawing and a little packet of art supplies to take home. My greatest concern is that children in my home learn that God wants them to know him and that we can each have a relationship with him.

A Prayer

Dear Lord, I know kids are like sponges. I know they are affected by what they read and what they see in movies. Please protect their hearts and minds. You tell us that you send us out among the wolves. Please help these little ones to be wise as serpents and harmless as doves. Amen.

CHAPTER

EIGHT

"W" Stands for "Who Knows What?"

Is Mary Magdalene in The Last Supper*?*

". . . each of them began to say to Him, 'Lord, is it I?' "

—MARK 14:19 (KJV)

LAURA AND LING came in for just a cup of coffee before driving home. On this last day of art class no one wanted to say good-bye, but we were tired from painting all morning. A huge poster of Leonardo da Vinci's *The Last Supper* and notes were scattered all over the kitchen table.

"Look, Ling!" Laura moved quickly to the table. "It's beautiful!"

"If you could just learn to paint like Leonardo, Gini!"

I filled three mugs. Ling strained her eyes. "It's so messed up from war damage, it's hard to really imagine what it would have been like in its day. It's not much of a masterpiece now."

"Not a masterpiece! What are you saying? It's the most internationally famous work of art in the world! Oh, thanks." Steaming cup in her hand, Laura stationed herself over the poster. "Do you realize this one work represents the 'central point of the Christian doctrine of salvation, the institution of the Eucharist?' "[44]

Ling grinned. "You've got some things to learn, Laura. First of all, this is not just a picture of thirteen men! According to Dan Brown in *The Da Vinci Code*, this is a painting to help us identify Jesus' *favorite* disciple, Mary."

"What? Mary? Mary his mother?"

"No, Mary Magdalene, his wife. In *The Da Vinci Code*, Dan Brown proves it."

"Gini, is that really what the book says?"

I thumbed through my book. "Yes, Ling's right about *The Da Vinci Code.* Right here. Read page 243."

Mary Magdalene: A Disciple?

The following is excerpted from page 243 of *The Da Vinci Code*

". . . The Last Supper is a painting of thirteen men."

"Is it?" Teabing arched his eyebrows. "Take a closer look."

Uncertain, Sophie made her way closer to the painting, scanning the thirteen figures—Jesus Christ in the middle, six disciples on his left, and six on his right. "They're all men," she confirmed.

"Oh?" Teabing said. "How about the one seated in the place of honor, at the right hand of the Lord?"

Sophie examined the figure to Jesus' immediate right, focusing in. As she studied the person's face and body, a wave of astonishment rose within her. The individual had flowing red hair, delicate folded hands, and the hint of a bosom. It was, without a doubt . . . female.

"That, my dear," Teabing replied, "is Mary Magdalene."[45]

Laura leaned over the painting again. "Look, Ling. John, or as you say, 'Mary,' has no breasts. The men all look quite similar to me."

I tried to help. "Several sources I read said that the men are painted in types. Other famous artists of the time such as Fra Filippo Lippi, Castagno, Donatello, and Ghiberti, stylized their characters this way. The elders were painted as old men, balding with only a halo of hair; the young men, like Jesus and others, were rendered with bright eyes, soft hair, and beautiful clothing like Christ in the blue sash; the scholars, younger than the others, had no beards. Their faces seem soft. They appear open like the one to the left of Jesus pointing to himself, Philip, as well as John to Jesus' right."

Laura counted, "Ten, eleven? Okay, and if that guy is a woman, where's the twelfth disciple, Ling?"

"Maybe Judas is gone. He's already out getting the soldiers."

"No, this has to be Judas," Laura announced proudly. "There's the money bag right there in his hand. Remember, he's the treasurer of the group. So where is number twelve, smarty?"

"Well, somebody had to take the picture!" Ling smiled at her own joke.

"Now look at the table." I joined the fun. "Where's the chalice?"

Laura followed along. "I don't see a chalice. There are only half full glasses and chunks of half-eaten bread. No chalice. Why is that?"

"There may be no gold cup, but there *is* a chalice," laughed Ling.

"Where? I don't see one."

"The answer is in the code—Da Vinci's code! Watch, I'll show you. First of all, see the giant *M* in the painting?" Ling traced an imaginary *M* going up John's (or *Mary*'s) right arm, down his left, up Jesus' right arm and down his left. "Right here. The *M* stands for *Mary Magdalene* and for *Marriage*!"

Laura was dumbfounded, "You've got to be kidding!"

"No, wait! That's only part of the message," Ling's face radiated a huge smile. She was really enjoying herself. "Look carefully, Laura. See the *V* in the middle of the *M*? Right here between Jesus and Mary. See here where their elbows and hips are joined? That's the *V*.

The chalice!" She waited for full effect. "That *V,* of course, in the shape of the cup, is a symbol for the holy chalice, which proves that *Mary Magdalene* is the chalice!"

"What? I mean if Mary were at the table, why would she be the chalice? Gini?" Laura turned to me for help, but Ling was quick.

"Because Mary Magdalene was actually the wife of Jesus. And since she was his wife, her womb is where God carried his bloodline. His child was preserved through Mary even though he went to the cross."

"What on earth are you talking about?" Laura glanced at the painting again. "Mary Magdalene was pregnant with Jesus' baby when he was crucified? You're insane! You really don't believe that nonsense, do you, Ling?"

Ling tapped on the cover of *The Da Vinci Code.* "Well, it says so in this here book!"

"You're crazy, Ling!" She lovingly slapped Ling's arm. "All that from a novel. Unreal!"

We laughed as Laura shook her head.

Ling loved the audience. "Wait! I'm getting something else. Maybe it isn't an *M*! I see, instead, a *W.*" She traced down John's arm, up Jesus' right arm, down his left and up toward the next disciple. "Yep. It's a *W,* which stands for . . . *who knows what*!"

They were feeling comfortable and having fun. But I realized we were miles from the discussion I was hoping for. Silently, I prayed, "Lord, if you want this conversation to center on you, I need help. I can't get it going."

Ling headed to the sink with their empty mugs. "Thanks for the coffee, Gini. Hope your book gets published. We'll read it. Let's go, Laura. Gini's got work to do."

"Please, just five minutes more."

"All right." Laura picked up her sweater, but then folded it across her lap. "Gini, do you have five more minutes? Ling, we haven't even asked Gini about her book. We still have time! Do you, Gini?"

I laughed. Did I have time? That was why I'd dragged them in—just to see the painting and share with them what God had been teaching me.

"What have you learned about the painting as you've studied, Gini?"

"A lot, actually, but mostly from reading and rereading the Bible." They both looked confused. "How about another cup of coffee?" They smiled, both filled their cups and relaxed.

"I think God gave the real Leonardo da Vinci an idea without Leonardo's awareness. Look at the picture again. He actually did paint a message into his fresco. And he's done everything he can to bring the viewer into the scene."

"Why do you say that?"

"Well, first of all, the painting's scene is from the Bible, but he painted it as if it happened in his own day. Then the characters are life-sized, and seated on the far side of the table, so we can see them all. Leonardo has used an artistic device—making the disciples on the outside edges larger—and although the table is horizontal to the room, the perspective gives the viewer a sense that the ends of the table wrap in our direction, bringing us closer."

"Does he change the meaning of the Bible?"

"Not the actual message, but he does bring drama into the Scripture. The dinner is recorded in all four Gospels, and each story has unique, detailed thoughts that only the men themselves could possibly remember. Leonardo gives action to those thoughts. Let me read to you the scene from one of them:

> When evening came, Jesus arrived with the Twelve. While they were reclining at the table eating, he said, "I tell you the truth, one of you will betray me—one who is eating with me." They were saddened, and one by one they said to him, "Surely not I?" "It is one of the Twelve," he replied, "one who dips bread into the bowl with me" (Mark 14:17–20)."

"How did Leonardo da Vinci illustrate the Bible verse?"

"Actually, it wasn't just one verse or one story. *The Last Supper* compresses Jesus' three years with the disciples into that one captured moment."

"Jesus' statement, 'One of you will betray me,' lingers in the air. He avoids their eyes. Leonardo highlights twelve men who are suffering greatly at those words. See the tension in their necks, their hands, their eyes? Several are shocked. Some are confused about what they've heard. But each of the Twelve wears a unique expression. As I stared at the painting, I thought I heard someone's agonized heart cry out in a real voice."

Story from the wall

"What did the voice say?"

"Well, that's the story I want to tell you. It really comes from all the Gospels and takes a minute to relate."

"We've got a minute."

"Are you comfortable?"

The women nodded. "We're listening."

"OK. Imagine just one disciple's voice. Let's say it's John."

The scent of fresh bread tickled our noses. The wine was resting in the jug. We relaxed at the table, looking forward to this feast. Our voices mingled in companionship as we joked easily.

At a moment when everything was quiet, Jesus cleared his throat. "You've no idea how I've awaited this meal with you."

Smiling, we each breathed in and sat a little taller.

But Christ exhaled painfully. We looked quickly back at him. His hesitation was deafening. Our grins faded—and then all was silence. He quietly shared his heart. "One of you is about to betray me." His eyes were pierced with pain. He reached out as if to pull us closer to him. But we straightened our backs. Each man leaned away almost imperceptibly. Jesus' gaze dropped to the tablecloth, accusing not one of us.

Our minds screamed, *Lord, is it I?* Our thoughts raced, *Could it be me? Would I do such a horrible act as to betray him? Oh, it isn't that I couldn't, but would I?*

Pierced with guilt, my look flew to the others, hoping to place blame there.

Philip? Maybe it would be Philip, whose lack of faith was exposed just yesterday! Philip, our evangelist, years back, had immediately recognized the Messiah and excitedly brought his brother Nathanael to the Lord! But what about yesterday when he had let Jesus down? He had surprised and maybe even embarrassed Thomas, as well as himself, with his unbelieving words: "Lord, show us the Father and that will be enough for us." How could he disappoint Jesus like that? "Don't you know me, Philip, even after I have been among you such a long time? Anyone who has seen me has seen the Father. Don't you believe?" (John 14:8–10). Yes, Philip could abandon Jesus. But betray?

Or Nathanael? What about Nathanael? Early in our discipleship he had declared, "Rabbi, you are the Son of God, you are the King of Israel" (John 1:49). But was he dependable? Did Nathanael wonder if Jesus could read his thoughts later when Jesus asked, "You do not want to leave too, do you?" (John 6:67). That was another day, but what about tonight? Was there disloyalty in his heart?

Simon had already shown his double-mindedness. Who couldn't recall his shining moment: "Jesus, you are the Christ, the Son of the Living God!" (Matt. 16:16). Jesus even rewarded him with a new name. "You are Peter, and on this rock I will build my church, and the gate of Hades will not overcome it" (Matt. 16:18). But I haven't forgotten how only moments later, Jesus rebuked this same Simon Peter: "Get behind me, Satan! You are a stumbling block to me; you do not have in mind the things of God, but the things of men" (Matt. 16:23). So quickly our mouths and hearts condemn us!

Tonight, with guilt heavy in the air, one by one we asked, "Lord, is it I?" "Lord is it I?" (Matt. 26:22 KJV), each of us caught in the agony of his own doubts.

Is it I?

A few of us excused our guilty faces. Some demanded others expose their intentions. But I, John, sat next to Jesus. He gave me the seat at his right—the seat of honor. Why would I be there? Did he know my fear and hope to change my heart? I looked away and reached to cut myself a second piece of bread. The drink tasted so good! If only my hand would stop shaking.

Peter shoved Judas forward. Judas caught his balance; his hand and the fat moneybag slapped the table. Peter spoke past him to me. "John, ask Jesus to identify the traitor."

I hesitated. I could hardly do that! I knew what Jesus' answer would be: "Why John, of course it's you!"

But Jesus himself heard Peter's question and gently answered, "It's one who dips with me in the dish!"

My knife clattered to the floor! My heart screamed, *Oh, Lord! I knew it all along! It is me!* But the nightmare continued.

In the darkness later, I proved my guilt. You see, Jesus invited just Peter, my brother, and me to come aside with him and pray in the Garden of Gethsemane. He wanted us to carry the burden with him. Jesus was so overwhelmed and troubled that he fell on his face to pray.

He was in agony, but I was tired. I vaguely heard him call us to come to prayer. I didn't open my eyes. I ignored his call. Much later, he awoke me with, "Are you still sleeping and resting? Look, the hour is near, and the Son of Man is betrayed into the hands of sinners. Rise, let us go! Here comes my betrayer!" (Matt. 26:45, 46). And there and then, I deserted him and fled (Mark 14:50).

I've turned my back on him

"So, Ling and Laura, as you can see, Iscariot played the Judas, but John or any of the other disciples could have betrayed him by acting two-faced, putting him off, ignoring him, or even betraying him to the enemy."

"In the painting, notice how Leonardo has continued the line from the dining hall's rafters right into the room where the Twelve are seated. Leonardo incorporates the actual window to the left of the painting for the light source in the painting. Even the table setting and linens match those of the monks who ate in the dining room. The setting enfolds us: anyone—followers, disciples, Leonardo, the friars—and even you or I. And we recognize ourselves at the table as the traitor!"

"Oh, my!" Laura had tears on her cheeks as she whispered, "If I'd been there, I would have wondered the same thing. I know I've turned my back on him." It was silent a long ten seconds.

Then Ling exhaled loudly and stood up quickly, "Well, we've really got to go now. Laura, get your sweater. Thanks for the coffee, Gini."

"You two are the best. I guess I'll see you in the fall?"

"Of course. I wouldn't miss it!"

"Till September, then."

After they left, I kept thinking about Laura and Ling. They've both been religious at points in their lives. But today? After a woman's children are out of the nest and she is widowed and/or alone, her life may lose its glow. But even if our first love for Jesus has flickered, he still reaches out to us with steady love and light.

Then I thought again about the real Leonardo da Vinci. What message did he really intend with *The Last Supper*? For fifteen years, he sketched, recomposed, and resketched before he applied the paint to the wall. Why so long? Where was his focus?

Leonardo's notebooks show a love for science, not God. He studied and dissected corpses to draw more lifelike figures. Leonardo was interested not in religion, but making a living. He spent his free time observing, inventing, and sketching ideas for weaponry. He attempted to get funding for these projects, but he ended up taking painting jobs wherever he could get them to support himself.

He didn't see God as the creator of life. He wrote, "Nature, being inconstant and taking pleasure in creating and continually producing new forms, because she knows that her terrestrial materials are thereby augmented, is more ready and more swift in her creating than is time in his destruction."[46] He makes no mention of any kind of god and certainly no mention of a goddess, either. He seems to be more of an evolutionist attributing nature to be the power of formation. One scholar expressed the meaning of his painting this way, "Leonardo da Vinci himself, like most great painters, never made the slightest effort to explain this or any other of his works, trusting that other men too can sense things that lie beyond words."[47] Who knows what the painting really means? But I heard a message from the wall.

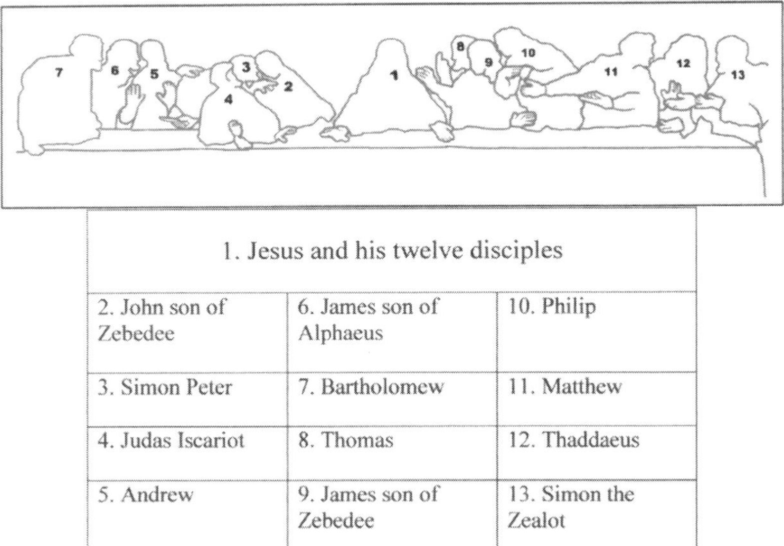

1. Jesus and his twelve disciples		
2. John son of Zebedee	6. James son of Alphaeus	10. Philip
3. Simon Peter	7. Bartholomew	11. Matthew
4. Judas Iscariot	8. Thomas	12. Thaddaeus
5. Andrew	9. James son of Zebedee	13. Simon the Zealot

Dan Brown says "M" stands for Matrimony and Mary	Gini and Susy say "W" stands for Who knows What?

CHAPTER

NINE

The Sacred Feminine

Are women holier than men?

"For you alone are holy."

—REVELATION 15:4

TWO COUPLES sat in a dark restaurant, enjoying a late-night pizza after the movie. "So, what did you think of *The Da Vinci Code*?"

Sara leaned forward, her eyes reflecting candlelight. "I loved that Sophie was secretly a princess. That's every girl's dream."

"Oh, boy. Here we go." Carlos, Sara's husband, rolled his eyes with a grin.

Sara laid her hand on his forearm and smiled, then turned and faced the others at the table. "I've always thought I was a princess, left to be raised by commoners, with the truth to be revealed in due time."

"You are a princess." Carlos cocked his head and then winked at his wife. As a newlywed, Carlos found her faults charming. "And that explains why you don't know how to clean the toilet."

"You are kidding me!" Jana exclaimed, ending with eyebrows up and mouth open. "My best friend doesn't know how to clean a toilet? Please! It's two simple steps—squirt and scrub. But maybe only us commoners can grasp the process."

"Babe, you're the queen when it comes to cleaning toilets. We do have the cleanest bathroom in the kingdom." Andrew picked up a fresh piece of pizza. "But I wonder, do you think Sophie was really a princess in *The Da Vinci Code*? I halfway think Langdon made up that whole story just to get her into bed."

"It's true. Women want men falling at their feet in worship," giggled Sara. "Try it sometime, Carlos!"

"I might, except that it violates the first commandment. You know the one: You shall have no other gods before me. Or goddesses," he added.

"Carlos, I don't want to be a goddess. Just a princess!"

"You are my princess, for sure." Carlos grabbed Sara's hand and touched his lips to her fingers.

"Save it for later, you two. You know, there is one thing in this movie that really confuses me." Jana twisted her soda glass, shaking it gently until the ice cubes clinked. "Langdon is a professor and he seems to know his history."

"He definitely does his share of lecturing," said Carlos. "For a while I felt like a paper was about to be assigned, due Monday."

"Wait a minute," Jana said. "Langdon talked a lot about women, and how their femininity and sexuality gives them a special power. I think he called it *the sacred feminine*."

The others leaned in closer, quiet now.

Jana continued. "He explained that there was a time when women were worshiped because having sex with them was a holy experience and the only way to reach God." Jana paused and rubbed her forehead. "But doesn't that turn women into objects? Instead of being elevated they become enslaved, useful to men only as a physical body, just a piece of flesh necessary to elevate the man."

Andrew broke in. "You have to admit, Jana, that there is a spiritual aspect to sex." He raised his eyebrows. "It can bring two people together on a deeper level than anything else."

"But in *The Da Vinci Code* it's a totally self-centered pursuit. The man is only using the woman to spiritually elevate himself. And that is the secret? That is what we've been missing out on for so many years?" Jana opened her hands, palms up.

"So much for being a princess," said Sara. "Sounds more like slavery."

Jana took a sip of her soda. She sighed. "I don't think the sacred feminine is the way to find God. There's got to be a way that's more fair."

"To women," added Sara, locking eyes with Jana.

The traditional household

Our culture sends us a chaotic mix of messages about the roles and responsibilities of women. I've processed through mixed messages since I was a child growing up in the sixties and seventies. I was raised in a traditional household where my father worked and made the money and my mother stayed home and kept the house. He was the boss, no question. My dad did the yard work and paid the bills. My mom got up early, cooked bacon and eggs, then cleaned house and took care of the kids. I don't think my dad ever changed a diaper in his life. I don't think my mom ever balanced the budget. They were happy, gender roles clearly defined.

Concurrently, however, the big wide world was overhauling gender roles. Feminism was blossoming, and I grew up hearing Gloria Steinem and other feminists poking holes in the traditional type of household I grew up in with observations like, "A liberated woman is one who has sex before marriage and a job after." Another even more pointed Steinem quote I remember seeing on bumper stickers: "A woman without a man is like a fish without a bicycle."

At home, my parents clearly appreciated and needed each other, but in school and in the media I learned that I could study any subject, pursue any career, and be whoever I wanted to be without needing a man for support. More radical feminists even suggested that women were better off without men at all: "Men are irrelevant. Women are happy or unhappy, fulfilled or unfulfilled, and it has nothing to do with men."[48]

My senior year at UCLA, I took a seminar on women's issues where the professor often lectured on empowerment. To me it was a new and intriguing concept that involved rewriting the roles of women in marriage, family, and society at large. While feminism advocated equal rights for women under the law in education, work, jobs, and pay rates, empowerment was all about power. As a woman, I learned to pursue:

- Economic power
- Decision-making power in the household, the community, the economic markets, and the state (politics)
- Increasing self-confidence and self-worth

The sacred feminine

While feminism emphasizes equal legal rights and empowerment seeks an increase in economic and political access and status, the idea of the sacred feminine emphasizes spirituality, elevating the female to the point of being exalted as a goddess and worthy of worship. And the goddess is everywhere, according to *The Da Vinci Code*, if we only look carefully enough for her in art, literature, and music (p. 261).

Even Christians are intrigued by the sacred feminine. Not long ago I read a book on this topic by Sue Monk Kidd; she's the best-selling author of *The Secret Life of Bees* and *The Mermaid Chair*. Her memoir, *The Dance of the Dissident Daughter*, tells the story of Kidd's feminist awakening. She was a Christian raised in a traditional

Baptist home, as I was. She married a pastor, wrote for religious magazines, and then, in midlife, something changed. She awoke to feminism, rejected Christianity, threw off the restrictions of her life as a wife and mother, and began to explore empowerment, the sacred feminine, and goddess worship. Instead of worshiping God, Kidd literally began to worship the idea of *woman,* gathering with friends in a rock cave in Greece to chant and light candles to the goddess, the very embodiment of the ideal of femininity.

While I don't want to dance around a fire and worship Mother Nature, I do have to admit that there is something appealing about the thought of being worshiped. What woman doesn't want more attention? More love? More power? And therein lies the appeal of the sacred feminine; it's a reverence of the feminine to the point of worship.

Even more attractive, the sacred feminine/goddess is characterized by some of the best qualities of women: beauty, softness, creativity, nurturing, and fertility. An aura of mystery surrounds the sacred feminine, often depicted as a universal life force around and in us. Common names for this deity include the Goddess, Mother Nature, Ishtar, Venus, and Astarte. In *The Da Vinci Code,* Mary Magdalene represents the sacred feminine in her role as the Holy Grail, supposedly carrying Jesus' child in her womb.

As the ultimate representative of the sacred feminine, Mary Magdalene must bear a heavier burden than just Jesus' child; she is symbolic of redemption and holds within her the answer to the quest for truth. "The quest for the Holy Grail is literally the quest to kneel before the bones of Mary Magdalene. A journey to pray at the feet of the outcast one, the lost Sacred Feminine" (*The Da Vinci Code*, p. 307).

Later, as the Professor Langdon character actually kneels before the spot that holds Mary Magdalene's bones, he hears "a woman's voice . . . the wisdom of the ages . . . whispering up from the chasms of the earth" (p. 454). Whoa! As a woman, I like the idea of being cherished and worshiped, but I'm not so sure that on my own I would consider myself holy or sacred, or that I want the responsibility for making anyone else holy. There is a heaviness, an overwhelming burden, that comes with serving as the vehicle for someone else's redemption. There's no freedom there. Like Sara said in the opening story, identifying with the sacred feminine sounds more like slavery than equality or empowerment.

A heavy responsibility

All humanity has a common quest: the search for meaning and purpose. When the search is successful, there is wholeness, satisfaction, and peace. When the search is unsuccessful, there is confusion, anguish, and despair.

Many spend their whole lives in the quest for purpose; in *The Da Vinci Code*, Dan Brown suggests that the possibility of success rests in the hands of women. He goes on to claim that the act of sexual intercourse provides enlightenment and salvation, bridging the gap between heaven and earth.

> Historically, intercourse was the act through which male and female experienced God. The ancients believed that the male was spiritually incomplete until he had carnal knowledge of the Sacred Feminine. Physical union with the female remained the sole means through which man could become spiritually complete and ultimately achieve gnosis—knowledge of the divine. Since the days of Isis, sex rites had been considered man's only bridge from earth to heaven.
>
> —*The Da Vinci Code,* p. 308

If *The Da Vinci Code* is right, women face a staggering responsibility, and not one I'm eager to accept. Can it be true? Are women responsible for providing a means to salvation for men? Am I? Do I even want that kind of power?

These questions raised by *The Da Vinci Code* get at the very question of the spiritual value of women. Earlier in the chapter, two couples joked about whether women should know how to clean toilets and whether women should be worshiped. When you are discussing *The Da Vinci Code* book or movie, the idea of the sacred feminine may come up. Below are some questions and answers to work through so you can be prepared to talk about what it means to be holy; if women are holier than men; how a person achieves holiness; and what the Bible says about the role of women.

Q. What is holiness?

A. The dictionary defines holiness as "exalted or worthy of complete devotion as one perfect in goodness and righteousness."[49] To be holy means to have *perfect* integrity.[50] Integrity means doing what is right, even when no one is looking. Holiness, then, means to *always* do what is right and *never* break the law. So by that definition, am I holy? Here's a test case: I am currently embroiled in a conflict with a neighbor over a giant eucalyptus tree that overhangs our yard and causes a huge mess. He refuses to cut it down or trim it. My feelings towards him range from irritation, to anger, to disgust, to intense ill will. Those feelings do *not* include love. Consider Jesus' second commandment, "Love your neighbor as yourself." Do I keep that command? Most of the time. Do I keep that command perfectly? A definite no—not with the eucalyptus-tree neighbor. By the definition of holiness, I have failed. Soundly.

Q. Who or what is holy?

A. God is holy. He has perfect integrity all the time. The Bible says that God is holy in both the Old Testament ("There is no one holy like the LORD; there is no one besides you" [1 Sam. 2:2]) and the New Testament ("For You alone are holy" [Rev. 15:4]). There is no evil in him.

God's son, Jesus, is holy. He is the *only* holy human who ever lived. The Bible calls him "one who is holy, blameless, pure, set apart from sinners, exalted above the heavens" (Heb. 7:26). One of his best friends, Peter, wrote that Jesus "committed no sin, and no deceit was found in his mouth" (1 Pet. 2:22). Even Pontius Pilate, the Roman governor who sentenced Jesus to death, admitted publicly that he could find no fault in him (John 18:38).

Q. Are people holy?

A. No human being maintains perfect integrity all of the time. In fact, the first man, Adam, who lived in a perfect world before crime or criminals existed, could not maintain perfect integrity. He and his wife Eve chose to break God's law. Their choice brought sin into the world and sin is the opposite of holiness. Romans 5:12 says it best: "Therefore, just as sin entered the world through one man, and death through sin, and in this way death came to all men, because all sinned." The consequences of this lack of holiness are many: physical and spiritual death; separation from God; sickness; addictions; loneliness; depression; despair; and bondage to pride and selfishness. "Not only is our life on earth wasted as we live for self and selfish desires but the consequence is eternal separation from God."[51]

Q. If we are sinners, how can we achieve holiness?

A. God is holy and we are not. Our sin separates us from God. The answer? Having faith in God's son, Jesus, the only perfect man who ever lived. Because he never broke any of God's laws, he didn't deserve God's judgment to die. And because he was God's son instead of Joseph's (or Adam's), he did not inherit our sinful nature. "You see, at just the right time, when we were still powerless, Christ died for the ungodly . . . God demonstrates his own love for us in this: While we were still sinners, Christ died for us" (Rom. 5:6–8). Christ's sacrificial death pays the price for our sins and allows God to see us as holy. And the best news of all—holiness is free. God will give this gift of a completely new life to anyone who believes and asks. Jesus himself promised that, "Whoever hears my word and believes him who sent me has eternal life and will not be condemned; he has crossed over from death to life" (John 5:24).

Q. Are women responsible for providing holiness to men?

A. Women, like men, are incapable of maintaining perfect integrity all the time so they don't meet the definition of holiness. John, Jesus' best friend, explained that "if anybody does sin, we have one who speaks to the Father in our defense—Jesus Christ, the Righteous One. He is the atoning sacrifice for our sins, and not only for ours but also for the sins of the whole world" (1 John 2:1, 2). As a woman, I don't have to take on the burden of providing holiness for a man. I cannot, but thankfully there is one who can.

Q. Are women more holy than men?

A. No; since holiness can only come through Christ, then all of us, both male and female, have broken God's law. We are equally lost and need help. In Jesus' eyes, men and women are equal. Paul explains, "there is neither Jew nor Greek, slave nor free, male nor female, for you are all one in Christ Jesus" (Gal. 3:28). God loves men and women equally. The Scriptures promise, "if anyone is in Christ, he is a new creation" (2 Cor. 5:1). In contrast, certain religions, such as Hinduism and Mormonism, maintain that a woman can only achieve salvation through a man.

Q. What does the Bible say about women?

A. The Bible tells of evil women like Jezebel and Herodias, as well as women of great faith like Esther and Mary. Scriptures record stories of women who are mothers, daughters, queens, prostitutes, widows, and wives. Some are wealthy, some are poor, some faithful, and some faithless. In the Old Testament, Jewish women generally enjoyed more freedom than women in other nearby Middle Eastern cultures. Recorded there are women judges, teachers, and prophets. Many New Testament women were faithful followers of Jesus and co-laborers in the early church. One writer calls Jesus "the great liberator of women. No other person in human history has done as much to make it possible for women to realize their full potential as image bearers of God."[52] Jesus spoke directly to women in public at a time when women were treated as personal property. He had many close friends and followers who were women, and a woman was the first person to see and speak to him after he rose from the dead.

Sex is not the bridge to heaven

Remember the story at the beginning of the chapter with Sara yearning to be a princess? I believe that somewhere inside, every woman wants to be special, treasured, a princess. Another story . . .

Picture a princess. She is beautiful, with hair shining like the sun, eyes deep as a mountain lake, and lips red as a berry. A knight comes, riding a horse. A brave warrior, he is true of heart but raw and untested in battle. He loves the maiden, the pure and virtuous princess. He fights a dragon for her, shedding blood and drawing some, too. He's relentless; he never gives up. Finally, he overcomes the dragon and wins the heart of the princess.

It's an old myth, told again and again in stories like Cinderella and King Arthur, but there's some truth there. After all, "myths are stories which confront us with something transcendent and eternal."[53] The story of the princess and the knight reveals something very important and very precious to the heart of a woman—the need to be loved and treasured. The knight values the princess to the point of fighting for her and even shedding his blood. In his willingness to die for her, his sacrifice is the exact opposite of *The Da Vinci Code*'s claim that women must take on the burden of providing their bodies as a sexual bridge for men to access God. Instead, in the myth, the knight protects the woman; he doesn't exploit her for her spiritual value.

Sex has nothing to do with salvation, and everything to do with delight. Try to read the Old Testament's Song of Songs without your cheeks growing warm. God never meant for men to use women as a route to the divine, but for a husband and wife to become one flesh, heart upon heart, evoking the passion and longing that Christ has for his church. Husband and wife are equal but not the same, joining in body, mind, and spirit and reveling in the safety and the freedom of their love.

To Read

Women, would you like to explore what the Bible has to say about your mission and your identity as a true woman of God? Read *The True Woman* by Susan Hunt (Crossway, 1997), or *Redefining the Strong-willed Woman* by Cynthia Ulrich Tobias (Zondervan, 2002). Men, do you like the image of the knight fighting for the princess? Read *Wild at Heart* by John Eldredge (Thomas Nelson, 2001) for more on the strength and wildness of a Christian man. May God give you wisdom as you search for your true identity as a woman or a man in Christ.

CHAPTER

TEN

Plane Gospel Truth

How was the Bible put together?

"In the beginning was the Word."

—JOHN 1:1

THE PLANE JOLTED. I grabbed my sloshing cup with one hand and swept my notes and Bible into my lap and onto the floor with the other. My seatmate jammed her napkin into the spreading lake of Coke as it flooded the tiny table.

"Here, I'll call the flight attendant," she offered as I held the cup with my teeth and encircled the wet mess with my hands.

I grinned, my teeth locked carefully into the Styrofoam, "Danks."

"Looks like you scrambled and saved your work!" She laughed as she reached for my cup.

"Thank you, God," I breathed through pursed lips. I shivered thinking of the wasted hours from Dallas to somewhere over New Mexico if my chart had been destroyed.

"You've been so engaged, it must be important to you. By the way, my name is Chantelle."

"Hi, Chantelle. I'm Gini."

The flight attendant mopped up the mess with a wet cloth. "Sorry, but we've hit some unexpected weather here."

"No loss," I smiled to myself as much as to her. I breathed easier and began picking up and reordering the jumbled pile.

"Are you a pastor, Gini?"

"Retired teacher." Her shoulders lowered a good two inches as she relaxed. "And you?" I stopped shuffling papers, turned, and listened carefully with my best ear.

"I work in the dental field."

"In Dallas?" I questioned.

"No, I'm on my way home. Do you live in the Bay Area, too?"

"Castro Valley. And you?"

"I'm just over in Berkeley. My office is on College, just past University."

"Ah." I couldn't visualize where College crossed University, so I covered my ignorance with feigned busyness. I pulled out my Bible and began looking for where I'd left off.

I felt her glance over at my Bible. Immediately Chantelle buried herself in her book.

I went on with my study. I just got back into it when she interrupted.

"Excuse me, Gini. Can I ask you a question? Do you really understand what you're reading?"

"I beg your pardon?"

"I mean, I've tried to read the Bible—lots of times—but it just doesn't make sense. And besides that, it's boring. I mean, well, Genesis was kind of interesting, but then I got to . . . well, you know, the next book, and it was just a bunch of begats. I mean, do you really just read the Bible? Isn't it just a bunch of thees, thous, and laws?"

I grinned. "I know what you mean! When I first started reading the Bible, I had trouble understanding it, too. But then I got into one topic I really wanted to know about—divorce. My grandmother showed me her concordance and a topical index. Look, mine's right here in the back of my Bible. I looked up the word *divorce* and read all the passages about it."

"So what did you find out about divorce?"

"I found out God hates it" (Mal. 2:16).

Chantelle frowned and looked away. "Well, I'm divorced."

"It's not that he doesn't like people who are divorced; he just doesn't like the pain of it. In fact, he invented it" (Deut. 24:1).

"Really?" she stared back at me, unsure that I was right.

"It's true. Right here in Matthew 19:8 Jesus says, 'Moses permitted you to divorce your wives because your hearts were hard.' But he hates the idea of people ripping families and each other apart. He wants marriage to be a good thing."

"Well, that makes sense! Nobody who's been divorced would wish it on anyone else."

"You're right there." I figured the conversation was over, so I began scanning *The Da Vinci Code* for the Gnostic ideas I was contrasting with the Bible verses. She was quiet, but I could feel her watching me.

"Now there's a good book! Don't you just love it?"

"Well, it's interesting."

"What? Didn't you like it?"

"I thought it was a thought-perturbing mystery."

"Don't you mean thought-provoking mystery?"

"No. His characters' conclusions on the canon of the Bible and who they thought Jesus is, made his book into a fictionalized history. That manipulation made me frustrated—no, angry."

"Everyone knows it's fiction—actually historical fiction. So why get upset?"

"That's one of my reasons. In historical fiction you can count on the integrity of the events even though the characters and situations are fictitious. But in *The Da Vinci Code*, Dan Brown is not faithful to the truth of actual events nor to the historical figures that he uses to build his mystery."

"Give me an example."

"Okay. Look here on pages 231 to 234."

The Bible, Not of God?

"And everything you need to know about the Bible can be summed up by the great canon doctor Martyn Percy." Teabing cleared his throat and declared, "The Bible did not arrive by fax from heaven."

"I beg your pardon?"

"The Bible is a product of man, my dear. Not of God. The Bible did not fall magically from the clouds. Man created it as a historical record of tumultuous times, and it has evolved through countless translations, additions, and revisions. History has never had a definitive version of the book." . . .

"The fundamental irony of Christianity! The Bible, as we know it today, was collated by the pagan Roman emperor Constantine the Great."[54] . . .

"Constantine decided something had to be done. In 325 A.D., he decided to unify Rome under a single religion, Christianity."[55] . . .

"Constantine was a very good businessman. He could see that Christianity was on the rise, and he simply backed the winning horse. Historians still marvel at the brilliance with which Constantine converted the sun-worshipping pagans to Christianity."[56]

—*The Da Vinci Code,* pp. 231–234

Constantine and the canon

"May I?" Chantelle took the book and turned back a page and quickly ran her finger over it. "*The Da Vinci Code* here seems to record history like this: Constantine was doing his best to gather the books of the Bible together to unite people in Christianity. Is that untrue?"

"Correct, it is untrue. Constantine did *not* gather nor even collate the books of the Bible. He did, however, probably call the group of priestly scholars together to encourage the unification of Christians under Roman rule."

I could see Chantelle was thinking. "I've heard the word *canon*, but I don't think I really know what it is."

"*The Da Vinci Code* doesn't help; it confuses readers about what the 'canon' is. And actually, this word and the process behind it often puzzle even Christians. The word—canon—is a metaphor, a play on words. It comes from the Greek word, *kanon*, meaning a rod or bar, a measuring rule, standard or limit.' Eventually, the term *canon* was used to refer to the completed list of books given to man by God. Athanasius, bishop of Alexandria, referred to the completed New Testament in AD 350 as the canon. In other words, he labeled the collection of the twenty-seven books used in the New Testament as the final part of God's revelation, which had started with the Old Testament books."[57] However, this collection, this canon, did not begin with Athanasius nor Constantine."

"The actual terminology may conflict with *The Da Vinci Code*, but it just doesn't seem that important to me. I mean, it is just a novel. And the Bible is the Bible."

"But Chantelle, it may not be just a novel. I see it as a novel with an agenda!"

"What kind of agenda?"

"It plants seeds of distrust in the Bible. This vital point needs to be addressed as much today as when the canon was established: 'Whoever criticizes, questions, challenges, subtracts from or adds to the authoritative Word of God is ultimately undermining the divine authority of the Lord Jesus Christ and putting man, the creature in a place of authority instead.'[58] Listen to the point *The Da Vinci Code* comes up with:"

Jesus' Status Upgraded?

> The vast majority of educated Christians know the history of their faith. Jesus was indeed a great and powerful man. Constantine's underhanded political maneuvers don't diminish the majesty of Christ's life. Nobody is saying Christ was a fraud, or denying that He walked the earth and inspired millions to better lives . . . The twist is this . . . because Constantine upgraded Jesus' status almost for centuries after Jesus' death, thousands of documents already existed chronicling His life as a mortal man . . . Constantine commissioned and financed a new Bible, which omitted those gospels that spoke of Christ's human traits and embellished those gospels that made Him godlike. The earlier gospels were outlawed, gathered up, and burned . . . fortunately for historians . . . some of the gospels that Constantine attempted to eradicate managed to survive.
>
> —*The Da Vinci Code,* p. 234

"So, these gospels he mentions are the Gnostic Gospels that Constantine and those priests dumped as spurious?" Chantelle responded.

"Yes. Those supposed documents give information, according to *The Da Vinci Code*, that help us to see Jesus as more human. The books he says are gospels are the Gnostic Gospels."

"Do the Gnostic Gospels give more information about Jesus—information that we need to know about him?"

"I haven't read them all, but I've summarized the material in table 1 (Gospels Compared). Although these ancient scrolls include poems, myths, and mysticism for the most part, I find them to be fragmented, contradictory sayings that match neither biblical wisdom nor the Jesus we see in the Bible, at all. Here are three examples:"

- **From *The Infancy Gospel of Thomas*:**
  "1 But the son of Annas the scribe was standing there with Joseph; and he took a branch of a willow and dispersed the waters which Jesus had gathered together. 2 And when Jesus saw what was done, he was wroth and said unto him: 'O evil, ungodly, and foolish one, what hurt did the pools and the waters do thee? Behold, now also thou shalt be withered like a tree, and shalt not bear leaves, neither root, nor fruit.' 3 And straightway that lad withered up wholly, but Jesus departed and went unto Joseph's house. But the parents of him that was withered took him up, bewailing his youth, and brought him to Joseph, and accused him 'for that thou hast such a child which doeth such deeds.' "[59]

- **From *The Gospel of Thomas*:**
  "Simon Peter said to them: 'Let Mary leave us, for women are not worthy of life.' Jesus said, "I myself shall lead her in order to make her male so that she too may become a living spirit resembling you males . . . for every woman who will make herself male will enter the Kingdom of Heaven.' "[60]

- **From *The Gospel of Philip*:**
  "God is a man-eater. For this reason, men are sacrificed to him. Before men were sacrificed, animals were being sacrificed, since those to whom they were sacrificed were not gods."[61]

"Those are weird! You don't think anyone would take these seriously, do you? Jesus was not like these described—at least according to the Bible! They hardly seem a threat."

"You're right, Chantelle. And I doubt many people would even bother to look them up. But I think the problem comes in not knowing for sure that the Gospels in the Bible are true, correct, or complete."

"I listened to a very helpful audiotape by Erwin Lutzer on debunking *The Da Vinci Code* that helped me know that the Bible can be fully trusted. I came up with ten reasons from his tape. Want to see them?"

"Sure."

Ten reasons the Bible can be trusted

1. The Old Testament was authorized by God himself.

- Moses wrote all the Words of the Lord (Exod. 24:4).
- The writings were carefully laid in the ark of the covenant (Deut. 31:26).
- These Scriptures were kept and honored as the Word of God. Subsequent generations honored them (Josh. 24:26; 1 Sam.10:25; Ezra 1:2; Neh. 9:14, 26–30; book of Jeremiah; Dan. 9:2).[62]

2. Some literature of the Israelites was rejected because the people themselves had not honored it. For example, they had the Book of Jashar (mentioned in Josh. 10:13; 2 Sam. 1:18), or the Book of the Wars of the Lord (Num. 21:14).[63]

3. The early believers were careful which books they canonized. The following books were questioned through the years on the basis of suitability for canonicity. They were, however, included in the canon later because the picture of God and the main messages were parallel to the other Old Testament Scriptures:

- Song of Solomon (Song of Songs): too sensual.
- Ecclesiastes: too skeptical.
- Esther: no mention of God's name.
- Proverbs: some maxims contradict others.
- Ezekiel: too anti-Semitic; some verses lean toward the Gnostics.

4. The Old Testament canon was closed about 400 BC with the prophet Malachi, and as far as we know, was followed by 400 silent years.

5. The New Testament is accepted because of the character of God, not because of the cleverness of man. God has shown himself to be the Lord, who fulfilled the prophecies that were spoken and written concerning him centuries before he became flesh. Jesus the Messiah lived here on earth as the supreme Redeemer who paid fully for our sins. He has been faithful to every promise he has made throughout time.

6. The New Testament was written in a timely manner. Most of the New Testament was written during the last half of the first century. Most books were written to local churches (for example, Romans, Corinthians); some were written to individuals (including Philemon, Timothy); some were written to general areas with directions that they would pass on to others (specifically 1 Peter to East Asia; Revelation to West Asia; and Romans to Europe).

7. The New Testament was approved by living apostles. And as long as the apostles were alive, everything could be verified. "We proclaim to you what we have seen and heard" (Luke 1:2; Acts 1:22–24; 2 Pet. 1:16–18; 1 John 1:2, 3).

8. By the end of the first century, two-thirds of the New Testament Scripture had been deemed to be "inspired."[64] Not only did the common man of God accept it, but the book was recognized and used by the next generations after the early church, especially the apostolic fathers such as Polycarp, Justin Martyr, Tertullian, Origen, Eusebius, Athanasius, Jerome, and Augustine, who used and approved the whole of the apostolic writings.

9. A list of twenty-three of the New Testament books was published in AD 175. In AD 135, Marcian, an anti-Semite who rejected the God of the Old Testament, wrote a list that included only New Testament books that met his philosophy. The early church responded in AD 175 with a letter listing authoritative books. From this, scholars have identified a list containing at least twenty-three of our present twenty-seven books, as well as lists of forged documents ascribed to Paul. These were labeled forgeries.[65]

10. The content of the entire Bible supports itself as a whole. The sixty-six books written by thirty-three to forty-four authors describe the same Lord who eternally remains the same. THE LORD JESUS SAVES is the overall theme of each book. (See table 2.)

Chantelle looked up from my list. "The facts seem to be against *The Da Vinci Code*'s characters' assumptions. How can the book's characters say that Constantine set the Council of Nicea to do his bidding and then he closed the Bible's text? The church had already been using these books 225 years before then!"

"Not only that, Chantelle, but the topic of books of the canon did not even come up at the Council of Nicea. But the point is bigger: Dan Brown's book attacks the credibility of the Bible. *The Da Vinci Code* is no longer historical fiction."

"I think you're right."

No way could I understand the Bible

She was quiet for a long minute. "Gini, take me back to your reading of your grandmother's Bible. After you read about divorce, then did you just start hopping around from topic to topic?"

"No. Actually after that I decided to read a whole Gospel, Matthew, to see what Jesus said about marriage and relationships. When I started the next book, Mark, I was surprised. It seemed to me that Mark had all but copied Matthew. That got boring, so I skipped it. Then I went to Luke. It was a lot like Matthew, too, and I decided I was finished. I stopped reading."

"About that time, my grandmother asked if I understood what I was reading. I explained to her about my boredom, and she said she was surprised I had gotten that far!"

"Really? I thought you said she read her Bible."

"Grandma explained to me that there was no way I was going to understand the Bible until I became a Christian."

I showed Chantelle the passage I was thinking of. "The Bible puts it this way:

> The man who isn't a Christian can't understand and can't accept these thoughts from God, which the Holy Spirit teaches us. They sound foolish to him because only those who have the Holy Spirit living inside them can understand what the Holy Spirit means. He just can't take it in. But the spiritual man has insight into everything. That bothers and baffles the man of the world, who can't understand even what this spiritual man explains. How could he? For according to this, 'he has never been one to know the Lord's thoughts, to discuss them, nor, certainly, to have moved the hands of God by prayer. But, strange as it seems, we 'Christians actually do have within us a portion of the very thoughts and mind of Christ' (1 Cor. 2:14–16 TLB).

I assumed I was a Christian!

"So, Chantelle, according to this, people who aren't Christians can't understand these truths from God's Word. It all sounds foolish to them. Only those who have God's Spirit inside can understand what the Spirit means. Others don't and find the Bible confusing."

"Well, I don't understand the Bible. Are you saying . . . ? But, I *am* a Christian!"

"Maybe you are. When did you first believe that Jesus is the one true God?"

"I guess I've always believed in him. I was baptized Catholic when I was a baby."

"Were you such a tiny baby that you can't remember that day?"

Chantelle nodded.

"Then it must have been your parents who believed, and so they had you baptized."

"I suppose so."

"Do you remember another day when you accepted Jesus' salvation?"

"No. I just assumed . . ." She shook her head.

"Chantelle, would you like to make certain that you are a Christian today?"

"Let me check my watch. We land in twelve minutes. Can I become a Christian in twelve minutes?"

"If you have faith, anything is possible. Do you believe that Jesus is the Son of God?"

"I do."

"Do you believe that Jesus is God?"

"Yes."

"Do you know what sin is?"

"According to the catechism I learned that sin is inherent in man, it is his nature. It's also not knowing God, choosing to go against God's will, or transgressing his commands."

"Right. Are you a sinner?"

"Everyone is a sinner; no one is perfect."

"So that means you have a sinful nature; you're human. Have you sinned intentionally, too?"

"I'm sure I have."

"Think for a few moments. In your heart tell God that you know you are a sinner and confess, agree with him about any sins he makes you aware of."

After we sat silent for a few moments, I began again. "Have you confessed your sins to God?"

"I have."

"The Bible says in Romans 6:23 that 'The wages of sin is death.' Do you believe that you deserve death?" I scribbled the reference down on a scrap of paper.

"According to that verse, I guess I do."

"You guess?"

"No, I know I do."

I opened my Bible to this verse and pointed. "Romans 5:8 says 'God demonstrates his own love for us in this: while we were still sinners Christ died for us.' Someone had to pay for your death penalty, Chantelle. You were doomed—another way of looking at it is that you were already dead." I wrote this verse down, too.

"I can see that."

"Another verse," I flipped over to Colossians 2:13, "says it this way,"

> When you were dead in your sins and in the uncircumcision of your sinful nature, God made you alive with Christ. He forgave us all our sins, having canceled the written code, with its regulations, that was against us and that stood opposed to us; he took it away, nailing it to the cross. And having disarmed the powers and authorities, he made a public spectacle of them, triumphing over them by the cross.

"Do you understand what that verse is saying, Chantelle?"

"I don't think so."

"Here, you hold my Bible," I noted this one quickly and pointed to the verse, "and I'll try to take you through the passage thought by thought."

I'll try to say it in other words

" 'When you were dead in your sins and . . . your sinful nature,' means 'when you were already sitting on death row.' Remember reading, Chantelle, 'the wages of sin is death?' "

She nodded.

I pointed back to the Colossians verse. "When you were sitting on death row, because of your guilt—you were a sinner and you had committed the sins—God made you alive with Christ. He gave you the gift of life instead. Do you get the gist so far?"

"So far."

"OK, Chantelle. 'He forgave all our sins.' "

Chantelle nodded. "He forgave my sins."

"Yes. 'Having canceled the written code, with its regulations, that was against us and that stood opposed to us . . .' "

She frowned and shook her head.

"This word picture shows your prison door. On the door there is a piece of paper with your name at the top. Under your name is a list of actual sins you have done. The list yells, 'condemned!' God rips off the piece of paper and uses a big red pen to write 'paid in full' over each and every sin. You'll be shocked when you see what happens next, Chantelle. He walks over to the cross where Jesus lies. The verse says, 'He took it [the list] away, nailing it to the cross.' So I imagine, with your list in God's hand, he raises Jesus' hand just before the nail is driven in, then slides your list right under Jesus' wrist. God himself drives the spike right into his own Son's hand!"

"Oh, my Lord!"

"Yes! But the verse ends, 'And having disarmed the powers and authorities, he made a public spectacle of them, triumphing over them by the cross!' God sees the just punishment has been carried out by Jesus' death on the cross and both he and Jesus cry out in victory, 'It is finished!' "

Tears are on Chantelle's cheeks. "Oh, God!" she breathed. "Thank you!"

"Remember the first verse I told you a minute ago, Romans 6:23?"

Chantelle shook her head.

I turned to the passage again while Chantelle pulled out a tissue. "It says, 'The wages of sin is death, but the free gift of God is eternal life in Jesus Christ our Lord.' "

"Chantelle, as a dentist, when you find decay, you have to remove it, right? When it goes to the root that means a full root canal. But if God were the dentist, he would extract the tooth, the decay, root, nerve, and blood vessels. Then he would work a miracle. He would transplant in our socket a new, perfect, whole tooth—living, and complete; one that would never, ever decay. In other words, Jesus' life can be exchanged for our old one. Won't you accept what he offers you?"

She laughed. "I'd be a fool not to."

"Prepare for landing," I heard over her words. We buckled our seat belts and pulled our seats upright. We held hands while we prayed. As the plane landed, Chantelle knew she had accepted the gift of eternal life that God offered to her through Jesus' death.

"Where can I get one of those Bibles like you use?"

"Online, I'm sure. But I'd really like to give you one."

"No. Really?"

"Really!" I quickly signed and addressed the note with the verses. Then I scribbled her name and business address, as well as her e-mail, on a sticky note for me.

As we got our bags down from the overhead bins, we hugged. "Thank you so much."

Again we hugged, and off she dashed.

The last book

The New Testament Gospels we know today were written in their entirety and circulated as public domain at no more than sixty-five years after the death of Jesus. Jesus' witnesses wrote them separately as early as four years after the crucifixion. These testimonies were accepted as true by thousands of actual witnesses. Their testimonies were accompanied by the threat of death, and many thousands of believers were martyred as a result.

John MacArthur, author, pastor, and teacher, reminds us that in the twenty-first century, "The 'canon of Scripture' is a term all Christians should know and understand better. Since the close of the New Testament canon in the fourth century some people have wondered if we shouldn't be able to add to the canon. After all, God has continued to act and speak since those first centuries through the

Holy Spirit of Christ. But Revelation 22:18 clearly states: 'I warn everyone who hears the words of the prophecy of this book: If anyone adds anything to them, God will add to him the plagues described in this book.' Of course you can scoff and say this warning applies only to the book of Revelation, not the entire Bible. But before you congratulate yourself too loudly, realize that the book of Revelation is the last book of the Bible, by its very nature, by its content, and by choice of those who determined the canon. If you add to Revelation, you add to the Bible, and put yourself in danger of the curse in Revelation 22:18."[66]

Dear Chantelle

A week later, I wrote a note in the front of her new Bible:

> "Dear Chantelle,
>
> The Bible is the Word of truth. It is the key to God's thoughts. I know, Chantelle, that God will teach you about himself from it. I love this verse from Isaiah 55:10, 11: 'As the rain and the snow come down from heaven, and do not return to it without watering the earth and making it bud and flourish, so that it yields seed for the sower and bread for the eater, so is my word that goes out from my mouth: It will not return to me empty, but will accomplish what I desire and achieve the purpose for which I sent it.' "

The next week I delivered Chantelle's Bible, complete with a concordance and topical index in the back. We didn't have much time to talk, just a quick "How's it going?" But I know God will complete what he began in Chantelle's life.

A Verse a Week

In order to share Christ, we only need to know him personally. But the results will be in God's hands if we share the Bible. I need more of his Word available for God to use as I witness. I need to memorize more. Will you covenant with me to memorize a verse a week along with the reference of where it is in the Bible? I'll be keeping a recipe card with a verse on it in my pocket. How about you?

Table 1. Gospels Compared

TEXTS	THE BIBLE GOSPELS MATTHEW, MARK, LUKE, JOHN	THE GNOSTIC GOSPELS
Authors	Matthew, Mark, Luke, John	Anonymous or pseudonymous
Credentials	Apostles or those who knew apostles. Eyewitnesses of Jesus.	Gnostic Gospel authors lived from one generation to several hundred years after the time of Jesus. They claimed to reveal secret, authentic knowledge about Jesus. Many quotes conflict with those of the Bible record.
Accepted by	Accepted as authoritative by earliest Christian communities by second century.	Small Gnostic communities, but rejected by the early church leaders.
Number of copies	More than 5,300 Greek manuscripts, some going back to the second century, plus other early translations (Latin, Syriac, and Coptic) from different geographical areas. The most extensive historical archive of any ancient literary documents.	Thirteen leatherbound books were discovered in 1945 in Nag Hammadi, Egypt. These were written in Coptic, an ancient Egyptian language, though most seem to have been written originally in Greek. Also, uncollected fragmented copies from different sources.[79]

TEXTS	THE BIBLE GOSPELS MATTHEW, MARK, LUKE, JOHN	THE GNOSTIC GOSPELS
Date	Written from thirty to sixty years after Jesus' death and resurrection.	Written from AD 200–300, more than a century later than the canonical Gospels.
Reliability	Historians who have studied the four Gospels have generally judged them to be highly reliable historically, with stronger textual support than any other work of classical literature including Homer, Plato, Aristotle, Caesar, and Tacitus.[80]	Virtually no historians regard the Gnostic texts as containing any more than an occasional fragment of historical information, often paralleling the canonical Gospels. "The Gnostic Bible makes no pretense of being an actual record of events." Writers didn't believe any historical records of Jesus. These gospels are the thoughts of various teachers who were on a spiritual quest.[81]
Errors	Because of the existence of so many manuscripts and a century and a half of scholarly research, the four Gospels' texts are regarded as about 99.5 percent faithful to originals. Most differences are trivial. The only text variances that affect more than a sentence or two are John 7:53—8:11 and Mark 16:9–20.[82]	Existing texts are fragmented, rare, and cannot be cross-checked for accuracy. There is no evidence that they were ever known or recognized as authoritative by any other than a small circle of devotees. Those known to the broader Christian community were rejected.

Texts	The Bible Gospels Matthew, Mark, Luke, John	The Gnostic Gospels
Consistency of message	Each book has the same message: The Lord saves. Jesus the Messiah fulfilled Old Testament promises, revealing God as Father and bringing salvation by his death and resurrection.	Each author has different emphasis but the central focus is the same: "The most striking theme common to all 52 texts . . . is the rejection of the Genesis creation account." The authors mock Creator God as a blind fool.[83] There is no real historical narrative nor does Jesus die on the cross. Salvation comes instead by receiving secret teaching.
Goals of the authors	Writers' goals are to be reliable, clear, and accurate. For example, Luke wrote "I myself have carefully investigated everything from the beginning, it seemed good also to me to write an orderly account for you" (Luke 1:3).	Matthew, Mark, Luke and John were honest, even to the point of showing themselves as stubborn, ignorant, or even disloyal followers. Obviously not based on eyewitness accounts of Jesus' life, the Gnostic gospels are collections of sayings that share new, secret knowledge. Gnostics taught that the spiritually elite possess hidden knowledge of the divine that places their personal revelations, spiritual experiences, and interpretations of Scripture above the revelation found in Scripture.[84]

TEXTS	**THE BIBLE GOSPELS MATTHEW, MARK, LUKE, JOHN**	**THE GNOSTIC GOSPELS**
Who did they say Jesus was?	The Messiah, Son of God, the prophesied Savior of the world.	A demigod or supernatural being (rather than a mortal man), who did not die on the cross.
Salvation comes from . . .	Believing Jesus is the Son of God, accepting the gift of salvation, and embracing the values of God's Kingdom.	Secret knowledge granted only to a few who discover the "divine within."
Salvation is for . . .	Everyone who wants it. It's offered to the whole world. "For God so loved the world that he gave his one and only Son, that whoever believes in him shall not perish but have eternal life" (John 3:16).	The few who are worthy (or fortunate enough) to receive this knowledge or who are spiritually sensitive enough to decipher it.
View of the Old Testament	Affirmed it. Jesus quotes from twenty-four separate Old Testament books. In Luke 24:44, Jesus said, "This is what I told you while I was still with you: Everything must be fulfilled that is written about me in the Law of Moses, the Prophets and the Psalms."	Rejected it. God the Creator is often portrayed as "a fallen, wicked, arrogant being often called the *Demiurge*, or "maker," who falsely believes himself to be the only god."[85]

TEXTS	THE BIBLE GOSPELS MATTHEW, MARK, LUKE, JOHN	THE GNOSTIC GOSPELS
Goal of worship	To worship God "in spirit and in truth" (John 4:23). To glorify God and enjoy him forever (from *The Westminster Catechism*).	To celebrate and empower the self. With the correct secret knowledge, to connect with the universal energy of the spirit that is within every person.
View of women	Jesus related directly to women, treated them with esteem and received them as participants in God's plan. Example: "There is neither Jew nor Greek, slave nor free, male nor female, for you are all one in Christ Jesus" (Gal. 3:28–29).	"Simon Peter said to them: 'Let Mary leave us, for women are not worthy of life.' Jesus said, 'I myself shall lead her in order to make her male so that she too may become a living spirit resembling you males . . . for every woman who will make herself male will enter the Kingdom of Heaven' " (Gospel of Thomas).[86]

CHAPTER
ELEVEN

Jesus Is . . .

Is Jesus man or God?

"Jesus is the Christ, the Son of God."

—JOHN 20:31

CLAIRE NEVER hesitated to say exactly what she was thinking, so her faraway look and silence surprised me.

"Claire, what's on your mind?"

"So who is Jesus, really? Is he God's Son or is he God himself?"

I listened. I heard her, but I didn't respond. I wanted to answer *Yes. Jesus is God's Son and yes, he is the Lord God himself.* But in my mind, I could imagine it wouldn't make sense to Claire.

We are a group of friends who read together each week from *A Harmony of the Four Gospels.*[67] We had just finished the story of those muscular fishermen disciples reduced to fearful boys. Remember the day of the storm on the Sea of Galilee (Matt. 8:18; Mark 4:35; Luke 8:22)?

To me, it looks like this:

Disciples on the sea

The furious squall was breaking waves over the boat until it was nearly swamped.

"We're about to drown!" the men yelled at each other.

"Master, don't you care?" another shrieked.

Jesus was weary. The day had been filled with healings (including a demon-possessed man), confrontation by some Pharisees (over his identity and demands for a miraculous sign), an attempted intervention by his mother and brothers, teaching at the lake to a crowd (so huge he was pressed into a boat on the shore), instruction to his disciples and finally, a trip across the lake for the next day's challenges![68]

Jesus slept in the back of the boat, exhausted.

"Lord, save us!" someone yelled.

From the soaked cushion, Jesus quickly unfolded his languid body to a commanding stance.

" 'Master, Master, we're going to drown!' He got up and rebuked the wind and the raging waters" (Luke 8:24).

"Quiet! Be still!" (Mark 4:39).

I imagine that his outstretched hands seemed to flatten the roaring sea to slippery satin. The suffocating, hovering grayness rolled back, uncovering a billion sparkling starlights. Silence hushed all creation.

But then he turned directly to them. His deep brown eyes searched into their shocked eyes. Then he turned slowly away and they almost missed it, "Where is your faith?" he asked his disciples.

In fear and amazement they asked one another, "Who is this? He commands even the winds and the water, and they obey him" (Luke 8:25).

It's no wonder Claire was confused. Jesus' own disciples didn't know who he was, either! As Luke tells the story, he answers Claire's question: Jesus is the Father's Son, God himself, the Lord!

A reminder from your old English teacher

When an author writes, he uses three basic elements: the subject, the purpose, and the theme. For example, apply these components to the topic of food.

- The specific **subject** is "the Monroes' homemade bread."
- The **purpose** could be to *express* feelings (I love homemade bread); or to *explain* (let me share one childhood experience with the Monroes' homemade bread); or to inform readers (here's the recipe for Mom Monroe's homemade bread).
- The **theme** is the *message*, *claim*, or *main idea.* My message is "The Monroes' homemade bread helps bond the family together."

Compare the subjects

Although the Bible is sixty-six different books, the authors use these same three basic elements to tell their story. To begin, let's take just four books from the New Testament: the Gospels of Matthew, Mark, Luke, and John. Their *subjects* are basically the same: the life, crucifixion, burial, and resurrection of Jesus. But each portrays a slightly different view of him. These are the subjects summarized by Charles Swindoll in the *Living Insights Study Bible*:

Matthew: Jesus as the King, the son of David, the Messiah
Mark: Jesus as the Servant
Luke: Jesus as Son of Man
John: Jesus as the Son of God

The Da Vinci Code also uses Jesus as one of its main subjects. "Jesus and Mary Magdalene are clothed as mirror images of one another . . . *Yin and yang.*"[69] Could this possibly be? Could Jesus have been completed *or perfected* by Mary Magdalene?

The purposes

The purposes of the Gospel writers are expressed by Swindoll as follows:

- Matthew shows Jesus as the King, the son of David (Matt. 1:1), the very Messiah promised in the Old Testament.
- Mark presents Jesus as the Servant (Mark 10:45) who came to suffer and die for redemption.
- Luke paints a compelling beautiful picture of Jesus as fully human, the Son of Man who came to seek and save the lost (Luke 19:10).
- John presents Jesus as the Son of God come in the flesh (John 20:31), sent to do the work of the Father.[70]

The four biblical Gospels center on the same man—Jesus Christ—mostly during the same time period, his birth through his resurrection. Although events overlap, the Gospel writers describe the characteristics of Jesus. Some recountings overlap; others are unique.

This reminds me of an attempted murder case in which I served as part of the jury. Ten witnesses each described the incident through their testimony. Some saw the crime; some heard of it; all knew or had seen one or more of the people involved. The jury's job was to weave their individual stories together to determine the whole truth.

One possible purpose of *The Da Vinci Code* is to portray Jesus as "the original feminist . . . intended for the future of His Church to be in the hands of Mary Magdalene . . . the Holy Grail."[71] Another purpose could be to claim that the Gospels, the biographies of Jesus were rewritten. "Constantine commissioned and financed a new Bible, which omitted those gospels that spoke of Christ's *human* traits and embellished those gospels that made him godlike. The earlier gospels were outlawed, gathered up, and burned."[72]

The themes

Matthew writes to Jewish readers giving them absolute proof of Jesus being the promised Messiah (the Anointed One). Time and again he brings in not only Old Testament evidence of Jesus' heritage, but also his pre-Gospel existence. He begins his Gospel with the record of Jesus' genealogy directly from Abraham, the father of the Jews. The Pharisees are intent on disproving Jesus' identity as the Son of God because he interprets the law differently from the way they do.

One law from the Ten Commandments is to "Observe the Sabbath day by keeping holy, as the LORD your God has commanded you. Six days you shall labor and do all your work, but the seventh day is a Sabbath to the LORD your God. On it you shall not do any work" (Deut. 5:12–14). The Pharisees see Jesus and his disciples picking some heads of grain on the Sabbath because they're hungry. They accuse them: "Look! Your disciples are doing what is unlawful on the Sabbath," working by harvesting that grain (Matt. 12:2). First, Jesus reminds them of their precious King David who unlawfully took the consecrated bread from the temple for his soldiers and himself, and yet was not guilty. And then Jesus uses these Pharisees' own priests' work in the temple on the Sabbath as the logical answer to their accusation, "Haven't you read in the Law that on the Sabbath the priests in the temple desecrate the day and yet are innocent?" Finally he concludes, "I tell you that one greater than the temple is here. If you had known what these words mean, 'I desire mercy, not sacrifice,' you would not have condemned the innocent. For the Son of Man is Lord of the Sabbath" (Matt. 12:6–8). Then he refers them to the Old Testament verse of Exodus 31:12–15 and says clearly, "For the Son of Man is Lord of the Sabbath" (Matt. 12:8). Jesus didn't hesitate to let them know that he himself was the Lord of whom the Old Testament spoke!

I love the recounting Matthew does of Jesus' messages. In one situation, John the Baptist, who is in prison, is filled with confusion and maybe doubt. He is about to be beheaded. His life work has been to preach about the Messiah's coming and prepare people for this Christ. Now he has seen a Jesus who has not been the political warrior he expected. So, he sends a desperate message asking Jesus if he really *is* the promised Messiah. Jesus says this: "Go back and report to John what you hear and see: the blind receive sight, the lame walk, those who have leprosy are cured, the deaf hear, the dead are raised, and the good news is preached to the poor" (Matt. 11:4). This directly fulfills the prophecy of Isaiah 35, given seven hundred years before. John the Baptist would readily realize the fulfillment because he has been preaching the message just after this one about the highway called the "Way of Holiness" (Isa. 35:8). But more than this, the verse prior brings John hope with "Be strong, do not fear; your God will come, he will come with vengeance; with divine retribution he will come to save you" (Isa. 35:4).

Jesus served people by bringing healing, forgiveness, and encouragement

Mark shows Jesus' life work: serving others. It is written to the Roman believers, many of whom were being persecuted. Mark reminds these people of the hope they have in a Savior who brought healing, hope, encouragement, and forgiveness into a world where there was sickness, discouragement, and sin.

Mark shows Jesus' life as only one of the close followers of Jesus could, through face-to-face encounters. Jesus served with a heart for those who needed him. For example, Mark recalls a miracle that none of the other Gospel writers reported (Mark 7:31–37). Jesus healed a man of his deafness and also gave the man the immediate gift of speech. Those who have deafness in their families recognize the hard work it takes for one who has never heard to pronounce understandably. How exciting that Christ healed this man's tongue, his lips, the muscles of his jaw, his throat, his eustachian tube, his inner ears, as well as his brain immediately, proving that Jesus does everything well!

Jesus' mercy and power

Luke, a physician for the disciple Paul, gives the most specific and detailed analysis of the man, Jesus, as no one but a scientist could. He wrote to a Greek friend, Theophilus, "so that you may know the certainty of the things you have been taught" (Luke 1:4). He provides a doctor's account showing what a physician would notice most—the specific care that Jesus gave hurting and struggling people. Luke focuses on Jesus' mercy, compassion, and comfort.

Jesus as the Son of Man is powerful as a human, but as the Son of God he is mighty. He had authority over life and death. My favorite story that only the doctor tells looked something like this (Luke 7:11–17): A pressing, noisy crowd surrounding Jesus runs headlong into a sorrowing, mournful funeral procession. The flutes end in discord as Jesus assesses the situation in a moment. This devastated widow has now lost her only young son. His heart breaks with hers; in empathy he offers her unknown hope. "Don't cry, mother." (Are those tears in Jesus' eyes?)

Jesus turns to the corpse, reaches out his warm, vibrant hand, and authoritatively commands, "Young man, I say to you, get up!" Immediately the man sits up and speaks, as if he is surprised at their carrying him on this bier. (Wouldn't a striving physician love that story of his Christ?)

Jesus brings eternal life

John, one of Jesus' closest friends here on earth, wrote the fourth Gospel. John explains his specific purpose: "These are written that you may believe that Jesus is the Christ, the Son of God, and that by believing you may have life in his name" (John 20:31). John leads with his purpose in his very first words: "In the beginning was the Word and the Word was with God, and the Word was God. He was with God in the beginning. Through him all things were made; without him nothing was made that has been made. In him was life, and that life was the light of men" (John 1:1–4). John announces that Jesus is God Almighty.

John pictures a powerful God under control. Anyone can see the love of Jesus for the sinner in the story of the woman caught in adultery. The officials insist that a person caught in this awful sin is already judged by Moses' Law to be stoned. Jesus doesn't show anger; he doesn't raise his voice. Jesus slows the conversation down. He stoops and writes on the ground with his finger. He reminds them "If any one of you is without sin, let him be the first to throw a stone at her" (John 8:7). When they watch him, for some reason they are convicted in their hearts. Each turns away.

Then Jesus stands up and asks the humiliated woman where her accusers are. She sees they have left. God alone is now her judge. Jesus takes his rightful position as God, forgives her of her sin, releases her from her deserved judgment, death (Lev. 20:10), and dismisses her to live the rest of her life in newness. We, too, heave a sigh of relief. We realize that in the presence of holy God, we are guilty. But by his Word, by his death on the cross, we, too, can exchange our sinner's guilt and deserved death (Rom. 6:23) for his life. We can be free! Who would not choose Jesus' way when confronted with the choice of death or life?

John is consistent in reminding the reader that his writing is meant to bring belief in Jesus. Once we believe, our next step is to trust Jesus Christ alone for salvation and purpose in life. My favorite verses that exemplify this are from John 14:1–3, "Let not your heart be troubled; you believe in God, believe also in Me. In My Father's house are many mansions; if it were not so, I would have told you. I go to prepare a place for you, I will come again and receive you to Myself, that where I am, there you may be also" (NKJV).

In John 3:16, 17, John reminds us that "for God so loved the world that he gave his one and only Son, that whoever believes in him shall not perish but have eternal life." He wants us to have life forever. The verse continues "for God did not send his Son into the world to condemn the world, but to save the world through him." God doesn't want any of us to face judgment. He already knows we are guilty. Someone deserves death. So God has provided the only way to life in the face of our condemning sin. God punishes Jesus to death for you and me; Jesus died because of our judgment. Now God offers us the chance to live his life.

The Da Vinci Code: Was Jesus just a man?

In *The Da Vinci Code*, the character of the historian, Teabing, gives his take on the Council of Nicea and its supposed purpose:

> "Aha!" Teabing burst in with enthusiasm. "The fundamental irony of Christianity! . . . It was all about power," Teabing continued. "Christ as Messiah was critical to the functioning of Church and state. Many scholars claim that the early Church literally stole Jesus from His original followers, hijacking His human message, shrouding it in an impenetrable cloak of divinity, and using it to expand their own power. I've written several books on the topic . . ."
>
> "The twist is this," Teabing said, talking faster now. "Because Constantine upgraded Jesus' status almost four centuries after Jesus' death, thousands of documents already existed chronicling His life as a mortal man. To rewrite the history books, Constantine knew he would need a bold stroke. From this sprang the most profound moment in Christian history." Teabing paused, eyeing Sophie. 'Constantine commissioned and financed a new Bible, which omitted those gospels that spoke of Christ's human traits and embellished those gospels that made Him godlike. The earlier gospels were outlawed, gathered up, and burned. . . .'
>
> "What I mean," Teabing countered, "is that almost everything our fathers taught us about Christ is *false*. . . ." [73]

The truth is that no one upgraded Jesus' status. (See table 2.) The Lord Jesus is the same God from the first to the last, the Alpha and the Omega of time and eternity.

There's more proof

If these four books, the Gospels, were the only testimonies we had of Jesus, they would be enough. We would have testimony of four righteous men whose lives were changed because of each one's individual belief in Jesus and his decision to follow him totally with the rest of his life. However, we have much more proof of Jesus' authority than these. The sixty-two other books of the Bible, written by probably forty authors, prove that Jesus is not just the Son of Man, but God himself.

At the beginning of this chapter, we looked at the three components of a composition: the subject, the purpose, and the main idea. The subject of each Gospel was Jesus: Matthew (Jesus the Messiah); Mark (Jesus the Servant); Luke (Jesus the Son of Man); and John (Jesus the Son of God).

Check table 2. Scan through the "theme" column. See how the Lord is the subject of each book of the Old Testament, and that the Lord Jesus is the subject of each book of the New Testament? Jesus is the Lord of both the Old and New Testaments.

So, what's the theme?

Now we look at the theme (the message or the main idea). The theme of each one of these Gospels is basically the same: the Lord saves. The Lord God shows it in different ways in different ages, but his desire is to save men and women. Most amazing is how the Lord's prophecies, acts, and quotes are carried and interwoven from the Old Testament into the New Testament. His message has never changed! You can move from the Old Testament theme verse into the New Testament with a matching or fulfilling action or quote.

Using table 1, look at the first entry on Genesis, for example. The theme is "The Lord saves as the seed of woman, the victor over Satan." The Old Testament verse is Genesis 3:15. God says to Satan, "I will put enmity between you and the woman, and between your offspring (or seed in the King James Version) and hers; he will crush your head, and you will strike his heel." Your offspring refers to Eve's progeny; Adam is intentionally not mentioned. Jesus is Eve's great-great-great-great- . . . grandson! He is Eve's offspring (just like our grandson Luke is my own grandmother's offspring).

The first reference to Eve's offspring in the New Testament Gospel is Matthew 1:18: "This is how the birth of Jesus Christ came about: his mother Mary (Eve's offspring) was pledged to be married to Joseph, but before they came together, she was found to be with child through the Holy Spirit." The offspring is not called Joseph's son, but it is Mary's child!

The second reference is in Luke 1:35: "The angel answered, 'The Holy Spirit will come upon you, and the power of the Most High will overshadow you. So the holy one to be born will be called the Son of God.' " Jesus is God's son and Mary's firstborn (Luke 2:7 says "she gave birth to her firstborn, a son").

Studying further, the verse of Genesis 3:15 is fulfilled more completely. The enemy of God, Satan, made sure that God's Son was nailed to a cross. A nail was driven through Jesus' heel. But God deals with the enemy, Satan. God gives a deathblow to Satan's head, ensuring defeat by raising Jesus from the dead. Thus, Jesus won salvation for those who will believe. And one day Jesus will utterly destroy Satan (Rev. 20:10).

Jesus proves through his life, death, resurrection, and his kingdom to come that he is God. He has the same power that he did when he created the universe. He shows the same care and concern for the Jews, the people he chose to use as an "example" nation, who would be his own special people. He still shows his love and salvation for those who choose to make him the God of their lives as he did with people, even foreigners, long ago. He lived in complete respect and fulfillment of the Law that he gave to his people in the Old Testament times. He is still Judge of all and will come in power and will reign as King over all in the end times. Because he is fair, just, and righteous, he will punish those who choose to rebel against him.

The message of *The Da Vinci Code*

Ah, but what about the message of *The Da Vinci Code*? There are several, but I've picked three main points:

1. ***People should distrust spiritual authority.***
"Sophie said, 'You think Jesus Christ had a girlfriend?'
'No, dear, I said the Church should not be allowed to tell us what notions we can and can't entertain.'
'Did Jesus have a girlfriend?'
Her grandfather was silent for several moments. 'Would it be so bad if He did?' "[74]
2. ***Faith is based on make-believe. One can't prove the New Testament because it is a lie.*** This theme is rampant throughout the novel.
"There's an enormous difference between hypothetically discussing an alternate history of Christ, and . . . presenting to the world thousands of ancient documents as scientific evidence that the New Testament is false testimony."
"Sophie, *every* faith in the world is based on fabrication. That is the definition of *faith*—acceptance of that which we imagine to be true, that which we cannot prove."[75]
3. ***The Gospel truths are metaphors, imageries, allegories, or fairy tales.*** This last theme is popular in twenty-first century philosophies (like Joseph Campbell in *Power of the Myth*) and movies (*Star Wars*).
"The Bible represents a fundamental guidepost for millions of people on the planet, in much the same way the Koran, Torah, and Pali Canon offer guidance to people of other religions. If you and I could dig up documentation that contradicted the holy stories . . . should we do that? Should we wave a flag and tell the Buddhists that Buddha did not come from a lotus blossom . . . or that Jesus was not born of a *literal* virgin birth? Those who truly understand their faiths understand the stories are metaphorical."[76]

The Gospels: A myth?

The Da Vinci Code's Dan Brown has written a best seller, a mystery novel that storms the foundations of the Christian faith. Contrary to the book's claims, Jesus is not a fictitious character, nor only a man. The Gospels are not myth, although the mighty themes of God have been woven into the fabric of tales since man was created.

C. S. Lewis, the author of novels, poetry, fantasy, science fiction, literary criticism, apologetics, and children's literature (*The Chronicles of Narnia*), said that Christianity is not a myth, but rather fulfills a myth. "The heart of Christianity . . . the old myth of the Dying God . . . comes down from the heaven of legend and imagination to the earth of history. It *happens*—at a particular date, in a particular place, followed by definable historical consequences."[77]

God has come to earth as a man as testified by the Old and New Testaments. John gives the theme of the Gospels best, I think: "Jesus did many other miraculous signs in the presence of his disciples, which are not recorded in this. But these are written that you may believe that Jesus is the Christ, the Son of God, and that by believing you may have life in his name" (John 20:30, 31).

Table 2. The Bible's Theme

The Bible's sixty-six independent books, written by thirty-five to forty-four people over 1,500 years, fit together miraculously into a library with a single subject: the Lord. With some study, you'll find each book has the same theme: the Lord Jesus Christ saves. The Old Testament section shows his birth, life, ministry, and death in prophecy, metaphors, and foreshadowing. In the New Testament, the Gospels show the Lord's actual life among us. The rest of the New Testament looks back to Jesus' resurrection and forward to his Spirit's work among the Jews and other nationalities, the establishment of the church, and the growth of individual believers. There are prophecies throughout, so far 100 percent fulfilled, which foretell his birth, death and resurrection as well as his future return. These sixty-six books are factual and true.

Old Testament

God chose to show the world his faithfulness through one people, the Israelites.

BOOK NAME	A THEME	A THEME VERSE	JESUS' MATCHING ACTION OR QUOTE
BOOKS OF THE LAW			
Genesis	The Lord saves as the offspring of woman, the victor over Satan.	Gen. 3:15	Matt. 1:18; Luke 1:35
Exodus	The Lord saves as the redeeming Lamb of the Passover.	Exod. 12:21–23	John 1:29; 47–52

Book name	A theme	A theme verse	Jesus' matching action or quote
Leviticus	The Lord saves through the blood atoning for sins.	Lev. 17:11	Mark 14:22–24
Numbers	The Lord saves life, demonstrated by the brazen snake.	Num. 21:6–9	John 3:13–15
Deuteronomy	The Lord saves as the promised Prophet.	Deut. 18:15–22	Luke 7:16; 24:19
BOOKS OF HISTORY			
Joshua	The Lord saves as captain of his own army.	Josh. 5:13–15	Rev. 19:11–16
Judges	The Lord saves from the cycle of failure.	Judg. 6:1–16	John 5:24–30
Ruth	The Lord saves by buying back his own.	Ruth 1:16; 4:1–9, 13	Matt. 16:18
1, 2 Samuel	The Lord saves as the rock, the true King.	2 Sam. 22:31–47	Matt. 16:16–20
1, 2 Kings	The Lord saves and his Kingdom will never fall.	1 Kings 8:58–61; 2 Kings 17:13–20	Matt. 10:28–40
1, 2 Chronicles	The Lord saves as the Promised King who keeps his promises.	2 Chron. 7:14	Mark 9:33–35; 10:15

Book name	A theme	A theme verse	Jesus' matching action or quote
Ezra	The Lord saves by directing the kingdoms of the earth.	Ezra 1:1, 2	John 19:8–11
Nehemiah	The Lord saves and unites his people for a cause.	Neh. 1:9	John 14:2, 3
Esther	The Lord saves by being a go-between.	Esther 4:12–14; 7:3–10	John 14:6

BOOKS OF POETRY AND WISDOM

Book name	A theme	A theme verse	Jesus' matching action or quote
Job	The Lord saves and is always sovereign.	Job 40:2–8	Matt. 16:21–24
Psalms	The Lord saves, is Savior, and worthy of all worship.	Ps. 22:1–31	John 1:51; Luke 24:46–53
Proverbs	The Lord saves. He is God, worthy of respect, honor, devotion.	Prov. 1:7	Matt. 16:24–27
Ecclesiastes	The Lord saves us for a goal; life without him is vain.	Eccles. 12:11–14	John 15:4–8
Song of Solomon	The Lord saves us for a relationship of love, beauty, and commitment.	Song of Sol. 7:6, 7, 10–13	John 15:9–13

Book name	A theme	A theme verse	Jesus' matching action or quote
Prophets: The Lord saves. He is coming as the Prince of Peace.			
Major Prophets (longer books of prophecies)			
Isaiah	The Lord who saves comes as Prince of Peace with judgment and consolation.	Isa. 9:6, 7	Matt. 24:30, 31
Jeremiah	The Lord saves, but judgment is near for all who do not repent.	Jer. 2:19; 9:23, 24	John 3:31–36
Lamentations	The Lord saves, with this Prince of Peace lamenting Jerusalem's fall.	Lam. 2:5; 3:22, 23	Matt. 23:37, 38
Ezekiel	The Lord saves. He judges rightly and tears down, but he will also restore Israel; nothing is impossible for him.	Ezek. 37:9–14	Luke 24:44–48
Daniel	The Lord saves by revealing prophecy of the end time of the world.	Dan. 2:20–22; 12:1–3	Rev. 19–22 (esp. 19:4–18)
Minor Prophets (shorter books of prophecies)			
Hosea	The Lord saves, but also judges, condemns, and punishes his people, all in his love.	Hosea 6:4–6	Luke 11:9, 10; 39–52

Book name	A theme	A theme verse	Jesus' matching action or quote
Joel	The Lord saves but also reveals foreign invasions.	Joel 2:10–14	Matt. 10:26–39
Amos	The Lord saves while revealing judgments against Israel.	Amos 5:14–27	Mark 7:5–16, 24–30
Obadiah	The Lord saves while revealing judgment against pride.	Obad. 3, 4	Matt. 12:22–32
Jonah	The Lord saves and renews after repentance.	Jonah 3:8–10	Matt. 12:38–41
Micah	The Lord saves as he warns of approaching judgment.	Mic. 7:18–20	Matt. 13:36–43
Nahum	The Lord saves, showing his faithfulness to his promises and judgments.	Nah. 1:2, 3, 7, 8	Matt. 20:17–19; 26:46–54; 28:6
Habakkuk	The Lord saves while allowing questioning of approaching judgment; he teaches that the just shall live by faith.	Hab. 3:11–13; 17–19	John 3:16–21

Book name	A theme	A theme verse	Jesus' matching action or quote
Zephaniah	The Lord saves while prophesying judgment and blessing.	Zeph. 2:1–3	Matt. 11:20–30
Haggai	The Lord saves while restructuring his house.	Hag. 1:7–9	Matt. 21:12–16
Zechariah	The Lord saves and calls for preparation for his coming.	Zech. 9:9–11	Luke 19:35–45
Malachi	The Lord saves and exalts the humble; he curses hypocrites and false teachers.	Mal. 2:7, 8, 11, 14, 15	Matt. 23:1–36

New Testament

The Lord proves his faithfulness through Jesus' life, death, resurrection; he establishes his Holy Spirit's presence in his people.

Book name	A theme	A theme verse(s)
GOSPELS		
Matthew	Jesus proves he is the Lord, the Everlasting, the King who saves.	Matt. 27:11; 28:18–20
Mark	Jesus lives and dies as the Suffering Saving Servant; he is the Lord.	Mark 10:45

BOOK NAME	A THEME	A THEME VERSE(S)
Luke	Jesus proves he is the Savior, the Son of Man, Lord of all.	Luke 10:9, 10
John	Jesus proves he is the Lord, the divine Son of God who saves.	John 1:1–3, 10, 11; 20:31
HISTORY OF THE EARLY CHURCH		
Acts	Lord Jesus saves, proving he is the empowering Messiah as the early church expands.	Acts 1:8–11
LETTERS OF PAUL		
Romans	Lord Jesus saves, proving he is the righteous Messiah, the hope for both Jews and Gentiles.	Rom. 3:21–26
1 Corinthians	Lord Jesus saves, proving he is the Messiah. The Lord gives the church instruction on the foundation, Christ, and on life through his Spirit.	1 Cor. 3:9–16; 11:23–26
2 Corinthians	Lord Jesus saves, proving he is the Messiah. He works through the apostle Paul's trials to God's glory.	2 Cor. 4:5–10
Galatians	Lord Jesus saves, proving he is the Messiah. Salvation comes through his grace rather than through our acts of impossible perfection.	Gal. 2:16; 3:2, 3
Ephesians	Lord Jesus saves and builds believers.	Eph. 2:8, 9; 5:1, 2
Philippians	Lord Jesus saves and shows faith at work through an imprisoned life.	Phil. 3:13, 14; 4:11–13

Book name	A theme	A theme verse(s)
Colossians	Lord Jesus saves as the all sufficient, supreme Messiah.	Col. 2:9, 13–15
1, 2 Thessalonians	Lord Jesus saves. He is coming. Be faithful in waiting.	1 Thess. 4:14–18; 2 Thess. 2:15–17
1, 2 Timothy	Lord Jesus saves and shows his faithfulness through a young pastor.	1 Tim. 3:14–16; 2 Tim. 3:14–17
Titus	Lord Jesus saves and teaches conduct for the church and its leaders.	Titus 2:11–15
Philemon	Lord Jesus saves and shows the importance of unity and forgiveness.	Philem. 10–12

OTHER LETTERS

Book name	A theme	A theme verse(s)
Hebrews	Lord Jesus saves as Messiah, the Superior High Priest.	Heb. 1:1–4; 9:11, 12; 10:5–10
James	Lord Jesus saves as Messiah, giving instructions on faith, works, the tongue.	James 1:2–8; 2:14–17
1 Peter	Lord Jesus saves, encourages, and comforts those who suffer.	1 Pet. 1:3–7
2 Peter	Lord Jesus saves, warning against false teachers and giving encouragement to live holy lives.	2 Pet. 1:19–21; 2:19b–22; 3:10–14
1 John	Messiah Lord Jesus saves and guides our fellowship with God.	1 John 4:7–10; 5:11–13
2 John	Messiah Lord Jesus saves, giving encouragement to walk in truth.	2 John 6

BOOK NAME	A THEME	A THEME VERSE(S)
3 John	Messiah as Lord Jesus saves, approving of Christian fellowship.	3 John 4
Jude	Messiah Lord Jesus saves and deserves glory and praise.	Jude 21–24
Revelation	Messiah Lord Jesus saves, returning as reigning, triumphant King.	Start with Rev. 1 and read through Rev. 22. Example: 19:11–16. Sources indicate Rev. 1:19 as key verse.

References

Nelson Pocket Bible Handbook (Nashville: Thomas Nelson, 1995).

Swindoll, Charles R., ed. *The Living Insights Study Bible* (Grand Rapids: Zondervan, 1996).

CHAPTER

TWELVE

Karen, It's Not Just a Novel

Does The Da Vinci Code *uncover spiritual secrets?*

"Every word of God is flawless."

—PROVERBS 30:5

NO! STOP! Listen! Karen, just listen to me. You just don't get it!" Crying, I awoke in the middle of the night. Why can't I get it right? So often, I end up arguing! Why is it so hard to talk to a relative about really important things? I know that Jesus wants me to introduce my family to him, but how can I share with Karen?

Yesterday should have been easier. We were only talking about *The Da Vinci Code*. Karen picked up a nubby scarf and touched it to her cheek. "Didn't you just love the book?"

"*The Da Vinci Code*?" I looked at her as I tried on some purple fuzzy gloves, "Actually, I hated it!"

"Well, I loved it." She smoothed the scarf back onto the bright stack.

I eyed her tenderly. "Dan Brown knows how to write an interesting novel. But he also takes advantage of people."

"Like how?"

"By *making* people think things about Jesus that just aren't true!"

"Be specific."

"He infers that God is complete without a female counterpart."

"I think the book is funny. Besides, that statement is no big deal; it's still a good book."

"Karen, it isn't funny! God is offended when we belittle him! It's sin! It's not just *nothing*. That's the trouble with people today who . . ."

"Stop, Gini. Breathe!" Karen smiled, inhaled deeply, and shook her head. "So what difference does what Dan Brown says make to you?"

I just stared at her, "What do you mean?" I felt I'd missed a step.

"Gini, Dan Brown can't make you think anything! Does the Bible say God was a man?"

"No, the Bible says God is a spirit and those who worship him must worship him in spirit and truth."

"That's what I'm talking about. You already know what you believe. And I know what I believe. So why make such a big deal over the book? Why can't you just let *The Da Vinci Code* be? It's just a novel!"

"Because it's not just a novel. Some people think it's true!"

"Do you?"

"No, Karen. I *know* it's fiction."

"Well, so do I."

I was getting hot. "It's an attack on God's character. It's blasphemous!"

"Well don't get mad at me! If you don't like the book, don't read it. Let it go. Come on." She had already gone three steps toward Cold Stone Creamery. Our discussion was over for that day, but it wasn't over in my head.

Historical fiction or fictionalized history?

The problem is that many people—even my Christian friends—dismiss the book with a wave: "It's just a novel."

There are two problems with that. Dan Brown has used a new twenty-first century literary device. Instead of writing historical fiction with real history and events revisited by fictionalized characters, he has written actual people (like Jesus, Constantine the Great, Sir Isaac Newton, etc.) and real events (Claude Debussy's death, 1918; seventh-century Vatican assassination of King Dagobert; Council of Nicea, AD 325) into fictionalized situations with new conclusions. It becomes fictionalized history!

But this second problem is more important. *The Da Vinci Code* is an intriguing mystery; it raises a number of important questions that need to be answered. I crafted the following double-edged questions for serious discussions. In *The Da Vinci Code*, Dan Brown has used a dangerous mix of fact and fiction. With that mix, most of the answers to these questions would be "Yes, but not exactly . . ." The book's answer would be incomplete until the qualifying answer could be added. Like *The Da Vinci Code*, other religions add their own philosophies, revelations, and revised truths to the sound doctrine of the Bible.

Q. Does the Bible really say Jesus was God?
A. Yes. (See chapter 11, "Jesus Is . . . ," and table 2.) Jesus says that he is one with God (John 10:30). God himself calls Jesus "God" (Heb. 1:3, 8). Jesus' disciples called Jesus "God" (John 20:28).

Q. Has the church hidden Jesus' true identity from people for centuries?
A. No. The last book of the Bible, Revelation, written around AD 90, refers to Jesus as God (Rev. 1:8, 17; 22:13). We still have that same Bible. (See table 2.)

Q. Are there spiritual secrets we have been unaware of until now?
A. Yes, but these are secrets about God himself. No one will ever know them until he chooses to reveal them (Deut. 29:29). However, everything is open in God's sight (Heb. 4:13). And Jesus didn't hold secret information. He said to a crowd by the lake that "whatever is hidden is meant to be disclosed, and whatever is concealed is meant to be brought out into the open. If anyone has ears to hear, let him hear" (Mark 4:22).

Q. Did God's priesthood include secret rites necessary for communion?
A. No, the rules and rites of the priests are completely disclosed in the Bible in the book of Leviticus. There was a closed place in the temple where only the high priest could go (Exod. 26:33). However, when Jesus (after his crucifixion) gave up his spirit, "the curtain of the temple was torn in two from top to bottom" (Matt. 27:51). From then on, the Most Holy Place was open and Jesus became our high priest. "Unlike the other high priests, he does not need to offer sacrifices day after day . . . He sacrificed for their sins once for all when he offered himself" (Heb. 7:27). Now we (who have accepted Jesus' death for our sins) "have confidence to enter the Most Holy Place by the blood of Jesus, by a new and living way opened for us through the curtain, that is, his body . . . let us draw near to God with a sincere heart in full assurance of faith, having our hearts sprinkled to cleanse us from a guilty conscience" (Heb. 10:19–22).

Q. Can anyone know if the Bible is complete?
A. Yes! The Bible warns "everyone who hears the words of the prophecy of this book: If anyone adds anything to them, God will add to him the plagues described in this book. And if anyone takes words away from this book of prophecy, God will take away from him his share in the tree of life" (Rev. 22:18, 19).

Q. Was Jesus whole in himself or did he need someone else (like Mary Magdalene) to complete his mission?
A. Jesus came to glorify God; that was his goal. Just before his crucifixion, Jesus prayed, "Father the time has come. Glorify your Son, that your Son my glorify you" (John 17:1). Concerning his life goal, Jesus said, "the Son of Man came to seek and to save what was lost" (Luke 19:10). He told his disciples, "the Son of Man did not come to be served, but to serve and to give his life as a ransom for many" (Matt. 20:28). In other words, his purpose was to die. He died alone; he didn't need anyone else to complete his mission. "Christ died for our sins according to the Scriptures, that he was buried, that he was raised on the third day according to the Scriptures" (1 Cor. 15:3, 4).

Q. Does Jesus have equal relationships with all his followers today?
A. There are certain men and women who are people after God's own heart as David was. God explains: the son of Jesse is "a man after my own heart; he will do everything I want him to do" (Acts 13:22). But the Bible provides this encouragement for all of us once we have accepted Jesus: "You are all sons of God through faith in Christ Jesus, for all of you who were baptized into Christ have clothed yourselves with Christ. There is neither Jew nor Greek, slave nor free, male nor female, for you are all one in Christ Jesus" (Gal. 3:26–28).

The personal connection

As for these important questions, I see several of these topics vital to Karen's beliefs. Her religion teaches that God did not give man enough necessary knowledge, so they have added other texts.

But the Bible says that,

> What may be known about God is plain to them, because God has made it plain to them. For since the creation of the world

> God's invisible qualities—his eternal power and divine nature—have been clearly seen, being understood from what has been made, so that men are without excuse. For although they knew God, they neither glorified him as God nor gave thanks to him, but their thinking became futile and their foolish hearts were darkened. Although they claimed to be wise, they became fools (Rom. 1:19–22).

In other words, everyone has knowledge of God through nature. Then it's up to that person to respond on that base level: we are to glorify and thank that Being, God. If we choose not to respond appropriately, the result is grave. God allows us to stay in the dark.

But here in the United States we have been especially blessed. We have more information available than just through nature. Everyone has been exposed to the name of Jesus. Churches are built every couple of blocks; there are radio and TV religious broadcasts; the topic of God is brought up in politics weekly; we are even reminded of God on our money! Practically every American has at least seen a Bible.

In the last chapter, we saw what the Gospels say about Jesus—he is God. We've already seen in chapter 10 what is contained in the Bible—truth. We've also learned that the Bible is a complete story of Jesus from the beginning of time in Genesis to the end of time in Revelation. And each book of the Bible contains messages of truth. When people don't accept God's truth, or suppress it, the result is "God's wrath" (Rom. 1:18).

I want Karen to have another chance to hear the truth. Karen is already in darkness because she hasn't yet learned the difference between the truth and a lie. She does not know the true Lord and has no relationship with him even though she thinks she does. Someday, maybe soon, she's going to need the real Lord Jesus. I want her to know God as her friend before death or tragedy catches her unaware. I love her and want her to know Truth.

Little Karen

Karen was born when I was twelve. My beautiful cousin was like the baby sister I had always wished for. I dressed her in my own beautiful lacy outfits Mom had saved "in case" we ever had a baby. I let her play with the Ginny dolls out of my collector's boxes. I snuggled her in a satin comforter and rocked her to sleep in our grandfather's platform rocker.

As a teen and a little kid, we threw off our shoes and waded barefoot in the gutter. With rose thorns spit-glued to our noses, we sneaked grapes off Uncle Fred's treasured Concord vines.

But as we grew up, our families became antagonistic over religion. My parents were agnostic; Karen's belonged to a predominant religion in our area; I was born again as a Christian. We barely saw each other when I was in high school and college. I married and moved far away.

Then a miracle! Karen and her family moved to a neighboring city only forty-five minutes away. I appreciate her now as a woman and hardworking mother of six. She loves her husband, adores her grandchildren, takes care of her aging mother, has a great sense of humor, and even, somewhat, looks like me. We go to lunch every couple of months. But we both know our belief differences are huge.

I know Karen loves me, too. Every once in a while, ever so carefully, she touches the borders of our differences. She searches for an opening to explain her church's beliefs. She brings up religion—not to win a prize—but to bring me a better life here and in the next world, she thinks. And she's wise. She never comes to the point of arguing, knowing that could possibly end the discussion and perhaps even damage our relationship. Above all, Karen doesn't seem to worry. In her belief system, I will have another chance. After death, her religion teaches, truth will be revealed to me (and others). Certainly I would not reject it then!

The real problem

But I am not so relaxed. I want to respect her boundaries, but I ache deeply for her and her family. I'm sure you have family or friends like Karen. They've added other religious books to the Bible, saying the

Bible is incomplete. So they have accepted a religion that adds continuing revelation to God's Word, then they reject sayings from the Bible that conflict with the new material. Thereby, they have changed the identity of Jesus; they've made him someone he isn't. I wonder if much of it has been unconscious and a result of their religious upbringing. But, what they don't realize is that the consequence of this rejection is God's wrath (Rom. 1:18).

Jesus loves my loved one

Now with this popular book, *The Da Vinci Code*, we have a false Jesus, a picture that is scripturally inaccurate. When a loved one reads the book and enjoys it, we may immediately assume that they will never get a chance to hear the real truth about Jesus. But you and I can relax. You see, the Lord loves them even more than we do.

> "For God did not send his Son into the world to condemn the world, but to save the world through him" (John 3:17).

In the past, I might have argued with Karen over our different doctrines, but I'd probably lose her friendship in the process, as I have with others. Now perhaps I won't feel the need. I believe God has given us a surprise gift with *The Da Vinci Code.* Because *The Da Vinci Code* surfaces topics that are common to many non-Christians, we have an awesome opportunity. We can make the book's characters, Sir Teabing, Silas, Bishop Aringarosa, Sophie, and Professor Langdon, our targets. They, after all, are the ones who hold these philosophies and methodologies so dear. We can use these characters as stand-ins for the discussions we would like to have with the member of a church who has a similar sincerely held religious belief. Following are some of the topics introduced in *The Da Vinci Code.*

Jesus' family

I would like the opportunity to ask Professor Langdon a few questions.

- You have become aware of some important religious news. With your discovery of Jesus' marriage and his clan's survival into the twenty-first century, what will this do to me? To start with, what are their plans? Have they composed interlinking family genealogies so we can determine who really is related to King Jesus? (Or who isn't?) Do these people have super strength or powers? What about intellect? How many are there?
- Of course this discovery will mean that one race will be superior and like gods. If I'm not one of them, is there any way I can gain worth?
- Does this super race have demigod powers?
- Will there be a huge change in the financial superstructure here on earth? Will those of us outside the family owe the others taxes? Will I still own my property? What insurance is there that my family and I will not be enslaved?

This whole idea is preposterous, but this super race is an actual religious belief of one of these churches I mentioned above! I'm thankful the Bible says "yet to all who received him, to those who believed in his name, he gave the right to become children of God—children born not of natural descent, nor of human decision or a husband's will, but born of God" (John 1:12).

Are rituals necessary to please God?

Sir Teabing, how would you answer these questions?

- What has happened to all those people between the time of Jesus' apostles and now who have had no opportunity to take part in the mystical union that could have brought them into harmony with God? Are they just out of luck and lost? What a tragedy for those who missed out!

- Without participating in rituals, can men and women experience the fullness of God?
- What if someone is not clever enough to understand how to work out a truth like this one? In one of the Gnostic Gospels, Jeshua [Jesus] said, "If you make the inner like the outer, the upper like the lower, [then] you make the male and female into a single. Then the male will not be the male, nor the female female . . . eye in the place of eye, foot in place of foot, and a hand in place of a hand, the image in the place of an image, then you will enter the Father's domain."[78]

Sir Teabing, the Bible says clearly that you can "believe in the Lord Jesus and you will be saved!" (Acts 16:31).

Where could the hidden documents be?

Any *Da Vinci Code* character, could you please tell Karen and me more about these Sangreal documents?

- How could these tens of thousands of handwritten pages that were supposedly hidden away in four large trunks be lost for so many years?
- Is there any historical evidence that the authors were actually eyewitnesses of Jesus?
- Were these documents written in the language of Jesus? If not, why not?
- Has anyone else besides one man ever seen the originals? What authority, reputation, and history does he have?
- Isn't it strange how often these very important documents of added religious material are hidden? Wouldn't it seem that those who have seen them and reverence them would want to share them openly with others, as well as put them into an understandable version?

God promises: "For you have been born again, not of perishable seed, but of imperishable, through the living and enduring word of

God. . . . the word of the Lord stands forever" (1 Pet.1:23, 25). What a relief that God's Word endures forever and is never lost.

I know that God wants my cousin to know truth. And I know Truth as a person, Jesus (John 14:6). I believe my cousin wants to know what is true. The Bible commands me in 1 Peter 3:15, 16, "In your hearts set apart Christ as Lord. Always be prepared to give an answer to everyone who asks you to give the reason for the hope that you have. But do this with gentleness and respect, keeping a clear conscience, so that those who speak maliciously against your good behavior in Christ may be ashamed of their slander."

Your friend is not the enemy

According to those verses, I need to make sure Christ is number one in my thoughts and my desires. Because I know him personally, I can spend time with him daily. He will prepare me for my actions and my conversations that day.

Then, I need to be prepared to answer questions, and I need to focus on what God would have me answer. I have found verses to study in my concordance under the topic of "Scripture." There are specific Bible verses I can share with those fictional book characters. I can even rehearse them. I should also expect that my friend may have some other questions, so I need to pray that I will hear God's answers during our discussion.

Further, I know I need to slow down and relax, and I need to discuss with the imaginary characters, rather than react emotionally to the moment. I must listen to Karen's thoughts and then in prayer, say only what God would have me say. Perhaps she will give me the opportunity to show her answers right from my Bible, so I should always have it in my purse when I'm with her.

Also, I need to remember that my cousin is not my enemy. The verse tells me to give my answer with gentleness, kindness, and softness. Being quick to cut down a person's response is rude. It also stops conversation and begins arguments. After an argument is over, there are hard feelings on both sides and the "clear conscience" is gone.

I need to guard against thinking that I am responsible for her thoughts or decisions. God does not ask that of me. He only asks me to have an answer for the hope that lies within me—not to worry if my cousin's answer is different. Praying for God to wake her up is the best tactic. He, after all, is God—and that my soul knows right well!

Send an E-mail

Dear Karen,

Hi cutie! How ya doin'?

I ache with you over your father's passing. What a wonderful uncle he was to me. You've taught me, Karen, through my parents' deaths how important it is to have someone who empathizes with you. I knew you loved me because of your calls and cards. We both knew their passing was expected. But death brings pain. And now that your dad's gone, I feel that same ache in my heart for you. You've suffered an attack by that old enemy—death! I know you need comfort, comfort only Lord Jesus can give. I am praying that you know his presence.

We haven't had lunch since before Christmas, thanks to my own busyness. Susy and I have been working on a book. This project has brought up a few questions I wish I could ask some of the characters in *The Da Vinci Code*. Maybe you can help me with some? How about next Tuesday? Looking forward to a fun time.

Love ya tons,

—Cousin Gini

CHAPTER
THIRTEEN

Take Time

Share your faith Jesus' way.

"I am the door."

—JOHN 10:7 (NASB)

I PICKED AT MY thumbnail as I nervously rehearsed my way up the sidewalk . . .

Good morning! Can I share some good news with you? God loves you and wants you to have life in all its fullness.

My stomach swirled in fear. It took me a good five seconds to lightly touch the doorbell. I heard a dog bark from deep within the house. I stepped back. Instantaneously, a young teen charged out the door. "Ma! Somebody's sellin' something!"

The door banged open. From Ma I heard, "Tell him I don't want nothin' and I'll sic the dog on him if he don't get off my porch!"

In panic, I grabbed the door and slammed myself out.

Here's life, America

In the 1970s, I was part of a blanket evangelism campaign called, "Here's Life, America!" In our church's unique four-week study program, we each memorized twelve verses.[87] I learned to read a little tract upside down. We had practiced for hours sharing the truths we believed with our whole hearts. We had prayed and prayed for God's Holy Spirit to fill us to overflowing so that we could share Jesus with our neighbors.

We had the phone company install twenty phones in our church gym. During the evenings, we telephoned all the homes in our area and made appointments with those who would allow us to come and share. On the weekend, we visited homes we had been unable to reach. It worked! We prayed with hundreds of people to receive Christ. We invited them to come to our church and we promised we would meet them there. However, we waited in vain for them to show up. Within two months, only one man was added to our church family as a result of the effort.

Quick-fix evangelism

Why was there so little fruit? We shared the truth; God's Word is truth. We kept this promise in our hearts from Isaiah 55:11, 12: "I send it [my Word] out, and it always produces fruit. It shall accomplish all I want it to and prosper everywhere I send it. You will live in joy and peace" (TLB).

God was faithful with his Word. At their homes, some people heard about a God they'd never thought of before. And those of us who memorized his promises grew in him. I learned that God had indeed given me his own Spirit to help me share with others. I began to realize that God was developing in me the desire to share who he was more and more—the gift of evangelism. I was no longer afraid to talk to strangers about Jesus. Those who listened heard a new hope for their lives. Unfortunately, within days, though, some also hardened their hearts against Jesus. The promise of an abundant and happy life dried up as they kept on in their same old lives.

Why it didn't work

What went wrong? Other churches grew. I've heard people's testimonies of becoming Christians from Here's Life America. Our intentions were so good! But our little church added only one. After all these years, I've finally spotted at least five problems.

1. Rewording Scriptures can be misleading, even scheming. My opening statement, "God loves you and wants you to have life in all its fullness," is a restated semiquote from John 10:10. The actual verse says, "The thief comes only to steal and kill and destroy; I have come that they may have life, and have it to the full."[88]

The translation of the verse I memorized says, "Life in all its fullness." This carries connotations of joy, peace, happiness, and maybe even wealth. Although God's "abundance" in our lives does indicate completeness and eternality, it does not mean that our lives will be without trouble. In fact, Jesus says, "I have told you these things, so that in me you may have peace. In this world you will have trouble. But take heart! I have overcome the world" (John 16:33). His believers are promised difficulties! So even in my first greeting, I was selling a product that I misrepresented.

2. Our team's focus was on quick-fix salvation, joy, and peace. One of the first questions I asked was, "God promises us a full and meaningful life. Why do you think most people don't have this abundant life?" In the campaign booklet, the next pages were about our separation from God: Romans 6:23 says, "The wages of sin is death." But I rushed on to the next thought, "but the gift of God is eternal life in Christ Jesus our Lord." I remember emphasizing the "free gift" to a woman who had read four pages from the pamphlet with me.

"So, what's the gimmick? Nothing's free!" she exclaimed.

"But it is! Just 'believe in the Lord Jesus Christ, and you will be saved.' That's a promise from Acts 16:31."

Belief is the gist of salvation, but paying for the horrible sin of our lives is in no way a freebie. "The wages," the payment, is still death! Isaiah 53:4–6 says it this way: "We thought his [Jesus'] troubles were a punishment from God, a punishment for his own sins! But he was pierced for our rebellion, crushed for our sins. He was beaten so we could be whole. He was whipped so we could be healed. All of us, like sheep, have strayed away. We have left God's paths to follow our own. Yet the Lord laid on him the sins of us all" (NLT).

3. Getting to a point of decision is not always God's immediate choice. But I wanted each poor soul to accept salvation and be saved. In my hurry to accomplish the happy ending, I made mistakes. Isaiah 55: 6–9 does promise that his Word will accomplish his goal. But what is God's goal for that person? These verses, in context, point to two huge errors I made.

> Seek the LORD while he may be found; call on him while he is near.
> Let the wicked forsake his way and the evil man his thoughts. Let him turn to the LORD, and he will have mercy on him, and to our God, for he will freely pardon.
> For my thoughts are not your thoughts, neither are your ways my ways, declares the LORD.
> As the heavens are higher than the earth, so are my ways higher than your ways and my thoughts than your thoughts.

Submit to God's timing

First, there is a specific time for each man and woman to seek God. We cannot push that time; it may not be when we have planned to be in the neighborhood. God breaks down walls people have put up; the Father draws people to himself (John 6:44). We don't do this work. So if I set up any schedule to win a person to Christ, my visit is not necessarily on God's timetable.

When it's his time and his way, his purpose will be met. I walk our dog every day on a trail above Lake Chabot. The leash laws are relaxed, so most people wander up the hill enjoying their freedom as the dogs sniff and scout to their noses' content. I see many of the same people, but not often because I walk at different times each day. I often carry my Bible or a pack of verses to memorize. Recently, I've toted along a copy of *The Da Vinci Code*. That time is time with God. I can sing, praise him, pray to him. I'm open to talk about God with anyone whenever God provides the opportunity. It's amazing how often people ask me about God. I think they feel safe because we don't know each other's last names. Besides, anyone can take off on another path at any moment. One woman asked me, "What does your Bible say? Do I have to confess every sin to my priest?" Recently, another woman who knew I was working on this book said, "Most of my friends already thought Jesus was married before they read *The Da Vinci Code*. They're almost relieved to find out it's true. Now he doesn't seem so godlike and they can relate to him better. Isn't that what the Bible is all about anyway?"

Second, people have to be willing to turn from their "wicked ways," and "evil thoughts." In the twenty-first century, *sin* is almost a forbidden word and almost everyone assumes their good outweighs their bad. A woman I've been sharing the Bible with said this: "I just don't understand why my sin is so bad. When my friend came to the Lord, there was a giant change—like black to white. But compared to him, well, I'm just a little gray." Of course, my friend knows she isn't perfect, but neither is anyone else! And heaven knows she has tried, and a good god would never send a woman like her to hell, would he? But I'm convinced when my friend gets a glimpse of a perfect God, she will fall on her face and surrender to him (Rev. 6:12–17), so that's my tack. However, back in the seventies, I was just worried that I wouldn't be able to remember the words I had to say to get someone into heaven. Now I understand that a person cannot be pardoned if they don't really want God's mercy.

Next, using a verse out of context can be misleading. A group I was connected with used these verses as part of a plan to share salvation with children. "Children, obey your parents in the Lord, for this is right" (Eph. 6:1), and "Obey me and do everything I command you, and you will be my people, and I will be your God. Then I will fulfill the oath I swore to your forefathers, to give them a land flowing with milk and honey" (Jer. 11:4, 5). This last verse is promised to the people of Judah. Neither is a verse about salvation. They give children a wrong view of salvation. First, salvation is never based on the right things we do. Even if we think we are good, our righteousness can never be compared to God's perfection. Neither does God weigh our good and bad on a balance to decide if we should belong to him or not. We are all sinners (Rom. 3:23). Secondly, this verse is written to a tribe of people, not to an individual. Third, we are not promised good land, food, or goods because of our relationship to God. We can expect difficulties if we are God's children, just as Jesus had to suffer (Rom. 8:17, 18). Christians are not guaranteed a life of wealth and ease (John 16:33).

I should have been using other verses instead. In John 9, Jesus is talking to his disciples and a man he had healed from blindness. The man did not know who healed him, but simply received the mud Jesus placed on his eyes and washed in a pool as directed. When Jesus identified himself, the man readily believed that Jesus was the Lord. Jesus went on to explain in John 10:7–11:

> Truly, truly, I say to you, I am the door of the sheep. All who came before Me are thieves and robbers, but the sheep did not hear them. I am the door; if anyone enters through me, he shall be saved, and shall go in and out, and find pasture. The thief comes only to steal, and kill, and destroy; I came that they might have life, and might have it abundantly. I am the good shepherd; the good shepherd lays down His life for the sheep (NASB).

This picture is of Jesus laying himself down in the place of a door. No one can enter except those he allows to come in. Salvation here is completely his doing. He shows himself to be "the way" (John 14:6) through his huge sacrifice of laying down on the cross, and nailing our offenses under his righteousness so we can have salvation (Col. 2:13–15).

We can't honestly close the deal until the whole price is disclosed. Salvation comes as a result of a process Jesus takes a person through; seldom can that be a onetime decision or prayer.

Think how hard it was for Nicodemus to understand spiritual rebirth. His journey started when Jesus declared,

> I tell you the truth, no one can see the kingdom of God unless he is born again. "How can a man be born when he is old?" Nicodemus asked. "Surely he cannot enter a second time into his mother's womb to be born!" Jesus answered, "I tell you the truth, no one can enter the kingdom of God unless he is born of water and the Spirit. Flesh gives birth to flesh, but the Spirit gives birth to spirit. You should not be surprised at my saying, "You must be born again" (John 3:3–7).

There doesn't appear to be any closing acceptance prayer. I believe Nicodemus escaped into the night, thinking long and hard about Jesus' analogies. However, three years later, in John 19:38–42, we see Nicodemus again, along with Joseph of Arimathea, a secret disciple of Jesus, beg the body of Jesus from Pilate, take it, and carefully prepare and bury the Christ in a new tomb. Somewhere along the way, Nicodemus became a believer.

Jesus' three-year program

If you follow Jesus' own disciples through the Gospels, you'll see the men that Jesus trusted most going through a series of steps in their belief. According to Orville E. Daniel's *A Harmony of the Four*

Gospels,[89] Jesus' own disciples had to grow in their belief in Jesus. This journey took about three years!

- ***Jesus asked them to come and see (Autumn, AD 26).*** After John the Baptist had baptized Jesus, John told two of his own disciples, Andrew and another (probably John), "Look, the Lamb of God!" They immediately followed Jesus. Jesus asked them what they wanted. Flabbergasted (I think), one asked, "Where are you staying?" Grinning [I bet] Jesus answered, "Come and see" (John 1:35–39 TLB). Andrew then brought his brother Peter to see. Jesus identified him without being introduced.
- ***The next day, Jesus said, "Follow me" (Autumn, AD 26) to Philip.*** Philip ran and got Nathanael. Jesus saw Nathanael coming and identified him as he had Peter. They all followed out of curiosity (John 1:40–50).
- ***His disciples put their faith in him (the end of AD 26)*** at the wedding at Cana, when Jesus turned water into wine (John 2:8–11).
- ***Again they followed him (Autumn, AD 27).*** At the Sea of Galilee, Jesus called Simon Peter, Andrew, James, and his brother John. "Come follow me and I will make you fishers of men." At once they left their net and followed him (Matt. 4:18–22; Mark 1:16–20; Luke 5:1–11).
- ***Matthew left all and followed him (Winter, AD 27).*** Jesus had seen Matthew sitting at the tax collector's booth. "Follow me," Jesus told him, and Levi got up, left everything, and followed him (Matt. 9:9; Mark 2:13, 14).
- ***They were identified as his disciples, learners (Spring, AD 28).*** Christ completed the selection of the twelve disciples (Luke 6:12–16).
- ***They didn't understand who he was (Winter, AD 28).*** "Teacher, don't you care if we drown?" He got up, rebuked

the wind and said to the raging waves, "Quiet! Be still!" Then the wind died down and it was completely calm . . . Jesus calmed the storm. They were completely confused. "Who is this? Even the wind and the waves obey him!" (Mark 4:35–41).

- ***Jesus asked them to clarify their commitment (Spring, AD 29).*** Jesus told them, "Unless you eat the flesh of the Son of Man and drink his blood, you have no life in you . . . from this time many of his disciples turned back and no longer followed him. "You do not want to leave too, do you?" Jesus asked the Twelve. Simon Peter answered him, "Lord, to whom shall we go? You have the words of eternal life. We believe and know that you are the Holy One of God" (John 6:53–69).
- ***They observed him in action (Spring, AD 30).*** Jesus arrives in Jerusalem and is hailed as King although the disciples did not seem to participate in this parade (John 12:12–19).
- ***They spent private times with Jesus (Spring, AD 30).*** Last Supper (Matt. 26; Mark 14; Luke 22; John 13).
- ***He helped the Twelve identify their fears and lack of faith (Spring, AD 30).*** On the evening of the Last Supper, Jesus said, "Do not let your hearts be troubled. Trust in God. Trust also in me." Thomas was so confused, he said to Jesus, "Lord, we don't know where you are going, so how can we know the way?" Jesus answered, "I am the way and the truth and the life. No one comes to the Father except through me. If you really knew me, you would know my Father as well. From now on, you do know Him and have seen him." Philip said, "Lord, show us the Father and that will be enough for us." Jesus answered: "Don't you know me, Philip, even after I have been among you such a long time?" (John 14:1–9).
- ***Jesus did not always get positive results (Spring, AD 30).*** Jesus was arrested. Then all the disciples deserted him and fled (Matt. 26:56).

- ***He called them on their lack of faith (evening after Resurrection).*** "On the evening of that first day of the week, when the disciples were together, with the doors locked for fear of the Jews, Jesus came and stood among them and said, 'Peace be with you . . . Why are you troubled, and why do doubts rise in your minds? Look at my hands and my feet' " (Luke 24:36–40). He rebuked them for their lack of faith and their stubborn refusal to believe those who had seen him after he had risen.
- ***He gave them what they needed (forty days after Resurrection).*** The disciples were filled with the Holy Spirit. They boldly proclaimed without fear to about three thousand people, "Let all Israel be assured of this: God has made this Jesus, whom you crucified, both Lord and Christ. . . . Repent and be baptized, every one of you, in the name of Jesus Christ for the forgiveness of your sins. And you shall receive the gift of the Holy Spirit" (Acts 2:36–38).
- ***And they devoted themselves to teaching and fellowship and to the breaking of bread and to prayer (Acts 2:42).*** They had really become Jesus' disciples. They were following, learning, and sharing with Jesus and others.

The disciples took a good three years to become believers! There were no magical moments when they could say that they became Christ's followers. Instead, it was a process.

A group on the Internet, referred to as the "Living Water," teaches would-be evangelists to use the method WDJD, or "What Did Jesus Do?" I like that. He took time—the whole time he had left—to bring these twelve men to a true knowledge of who he was.

This three-year program of Jesus with his own disciples illustrates our responsibility today for those who want to know Christ. Discipling is what Jesus did; he took the disciples into his life and shared it all with them. It was a huge investment, but it yielded great results: eleven for twelve. These eleven men became full-grown believers in Jesus. Would you be willing to let someone follow along with you as you follow Jesus to become his disciple?

The life of a true follower has a price. Jesus often reminded his disciples to count the cost. He was not surprised when many were unwilling to follow him, and he allowed them the right to their own decisions. In John 6:67, Jesus, seeing many of his disciples offended by his teachings, even asks the Twelve, "You do not want to leave too, do you?" Being a disciple is a tough fight. In Luke 14, Jesus reminds us that no king goes to war without a strong army. In verse 33, he warns, "In the same way, any of you who does not give up everything he has cannot be my disciple."

I believe in discipling. Charlotte and George worked with my husband, John, and me when we were in our twenties. Jesus discipled them and they mentored us. We spent at least one night a week with them, usually in their home. They were our good friends. They listened to us; they laughed with us; they studied the Bible with us; they prayed with us; they shared their victories and their failures in the Lord. We loved and we grew in the Lord together. Then we moved away and it became our turn.

That was thirty years ago and I'm still a firm believer in discipling. Jesus is still discipling me and so I'm mentoring Diane. She started her belief in the Lord three years ago at a women's retreat. She's a single mother who came from a tough life, but today, Diane loves the Lord so much! She has grown up as a Christian and is now passing her faith on to others. Each Sunday she serves on a worship team singing beautiful praises to her Lord. She works as a full-time secretary in a growing church. And she studies God's Word every week and is memorizing Scripture. She is still being discipled by Jesus, but she is also mentoring her own daughter and two of her friends in Jesus' truth.

A beloved pastor once said of discipling, "The fruit of a peach tree is not just peaches, but other trees!"

My Journey with Jesus

Studying Jesus' three-year program and the steps he took with his disciples was eye-opening. I've been on a journey, too. I want to write down some of the steps Jesus has taken to bring me to himself and to keep my own record of his faithfulness. What a wonderful treasure to hand down to my grandson Luke! Wouldn't you like to outline your journey with Jesus too?

—Gini

CHAPTER
FOURTEEN

Take Courage

Start up the hill . . .

"Fear not . . ."

—LUKE 5:10 (KJV)

IF YOU'VE DECIDED to take *The Da Vinci Code* dare and use the book or the movie to share your faith, we hope that some of the tips, techniques, and examples in this book will inspire and equip you to use the truth of the Good News of Jesus Christ to counteract the tawdry claims of *The Da Vinci Code*. Every believer who wants to share the gospel, however, will sooner or later face one rather difficult obstacle: fear.

Fear governs much of human behavior. Think about it. Why did you get out of bed today? Fear of losing your job or failing your class. Why did you take a shower? Fear of looking or smelling bad. Why did you drink coffee? Fear of grogginess. Why did you brush your teeth? Fear of cavities and bad breath. Why did you put on your watch? Fear of being late. Why did you lock your door on the way out? Fear of being robbed. Fear serves a useful function in that it keeps us from harmful choices and instead encourages good choices. There's nothing wrong with acknowledging fearfulness; it is a human trait.

Another human trait is our tendency to live in community. Of course some are loners, but by and large, people live in the context of marriage, family, tribe, neighborhood, club, church, company, army, or nation. And functioning inside a social network breeds a very powerful fear: *What will people think of me?* Asking that question stirs up a whole new vortex of fears, such as fear of failure, fear of rejection, fear of looking stupid, fear of seeming out of place, fear of being laughed at, fear of not knowing the answer to a question, fear of seeming weird, fear of losing a friendship, fear of offending someone you love. As you venture out to use *The Da Vinci Code* as an opportunity to share your faith, you will face some of these fears.

God knows all about your fears. Guess which command is the most common in Scripture? *Fear not.* God knows we struggle with fear, and that's why there are 366 "fear not" verses in the Bible.[90] Fear can be overwhelming and prevents even the strongest, smartest, most talented and educated person from fulfilling his or her potential. Fear breaks and freezes and strangles.

A fight with fear

Not long ago, I was watching horses on a hill. A fresh breeze tugged at my jacket. It was the first clear day after three weeks of rain. The horses charged ahead of me up the hill with an occasional twist and kick or a sideways flinging of the head transmitting their joy. They snorted, blown to life by the cold, clear air.

Later I drove down the coast with a friend. We were like those horses—joyful, free, exulting in open skies, green grass, and the run.

We had signed up for a conference at Mount Hermon, a place carved out of California's Santa Cruz Mountains just a few redwood trees away from the Pacific Ocean. We meandered down the coast under a blue sky.

We drove along, laughing and talking. I reveled in our friendship, warm in a magic, safe circle. We stopped at a beach where we got out and walked a bit. But it all went wrong. My friend fell off a cliff, breaking her leg, leaving a protruding bone. With blood everywhere, my friend was in shock. The ambulance finally arrived, whisking her away to morphine, surgery, and safety.

Shaking, I went on to the conference, the magic circle breached and my friend stripped away. I drove on to Mount Hermon alone. My hand-drawn map led me up a steep labyrinth of road cut through towering redwood trees. Onwards and upwards, I circled back and forth until I finally found the cabin. I let myself in, unloaded, sank into a chair, and wept. I slept fitfully, dreaming of feet slipping on gravel, ragged breathing, and cold rocks.

Night finally slunk away. I stumbled through the first day of the conference, still in shock. The day ended, and I had to walk back to the cabin, up the dark and winding road through the redwoods, alone and not sure I could find it again.

> Fear is a hill and
> I climb alone,
> trembling, weak,
> hard breathing.
> One thing I know:
> I can't go back.
> Home is up.

I started up the hill, praying. "Jesus," my voice cracked. "I'm scared."

There were no people or cars anywhere. Redwood trees leaned down over me, forming a tunnel of deep black thick with rustlings and whisperings. My skin tingled; my chest tightened. Emily Dickinson once wrote a poem about sighting a snake, and she called that chest-constricting feeling "zero at the bone." That's exactly how I felt; like my big brave self had melted away onto the road, and I now stumbled along on cowardly, zero-at-the-bone legs.

"Jesus, I can't do this," I whispered. "I don't know where I am."

Could I go back? Find someone with a car and nice, big fat headlights? No; the conference was closed, done for the night. Everyone was gone. I had to keep going. I knew I had to go up the hill.

In the Bible, wonderful, miraculous, incredible things happen on hills. Noah saw a new, clean world. Moses saw God. Abraham found a ram to take his son's place. Jesus was lifted up. And I had to go up a hill.

Broken and alone

But I couldn't. I stopped, the darkness wrapped around me, stealing around my soul like an icy hand. I couldn't move or breathe. In my mind's eye, I saw the horses again, necks arching, nostrils flared, galloping up the hill. They were free and beautiful and brave. I was small, broken, and alone, and I couldn't go any higher. Fear was winning.

Again I whispered, "Jesus, I can't do it. I need you."

Immediately I could feel him there beside me. My breathing slowed, my chest relaxed, the zero-at-the-bone feeling gone. I was not alone; I was walking with a friend.

The winding forest road grew straighter and not as dark, and Jesus and I walked up the hill. I began to smile as I remembered the old hymn I used to sing growing up: *What a friend we have in Jesus, all our sins and griefs to bear*!

I was never alone; I only had to ask.

Up, up, up we went. I stole glances at the small puddles of moonlight that filtered down through the trees, almost expecting to see him, but I couldn't. I listened for his steps, but heard only the forest. Somehow I knew he was there.

The circle of safety and comfort was back. As I reflected on the accident of the day before, I realized that Jesus is the friend who cannot be stripped away, the friend who will walk with me up the hill. Nothing can separate us from his love.

Perfect love drives out fear

I finally made it up the hill. It was a holy place. I started out alone, in the dark, not sure if I could go on. But I climbed it with my friend.

Sharing your faith can be like climbing that hill. You might be afraid because the map can be confusing, there may be unexpected twists and turns, it might be difficult to see the road ahead, you might feel very alone, and at times you might be afraid that you are not going to make it. But here's the key, no matter how frightened or uncomfortable you feel in sharing your faith: just start walking, one foot in front of the other, and Jesus will come and walk with you. And when he lights the path, fear melts into the shadows. "God is love . . . perfect love drives out fear," promises 1 John 4:16, 18. Love and fear—the two cannot coexist.

From fear to boldness

When I read *The Da Vinci Code*, I was first curious, then intrigued. Next, I got angry. Then, when people around me began to talk about the book and wonder if it was true, I felt the call to do something about it. At exactly the same time my friend and writing partner, Gini Monroe, went through the same sequence of emotions. She, too, felt the call to do something about this book. We created an interactive seminar for people who want to know the truth about *The Da Vinci Code*. Next came this book you're holding. It all started with the need to do something.

Scripture is full of people who received a call from God to do something, and what happens after follows a consistent pattern.

After the call comes fear. This is to be expected. "God has an inextinguishable habit of asking people to do things that are scary to them."[91] Some of the great heroes of the Bible, such as Moses, Gideon, Joshua, and Esther, were smothered with fear at the task God had given them. Even Peter, the Rock, and Jesus' right-hand man, was so scared that he abandoned Jesus at his moment of deepest need.

When Gini and I felt that we'd been given the task of responding to *The Da Vinci Code*, we both felt a great deal of fear. We prayed together often and continued to feel the tug to do something. With God's help, we decided to press on despite fear.

After the fear comes encouragement and reassurance. To reassure Moses, God turned his staff into a snake and back. An angel appeared to Gideon and reassured him, "The LORD is with you, mighty warrior" (Judg. 6:12). God sent Moses to "encourage and strengthen" Joshua so that he could lead the Jews into the Promised Land (Deut. 3:28). Esther was strongly encouraged by her guardian Mordecai to act to save her people when he said, "Who knows whether you have come to the kingdom for such a time as this?" (Esther 4:14).

A key source of encouragement for our *Da Vinci Code* seminar was the encounters we continued to experience with friends, acquaintances, and even complete strangers who were hungry to talk about the spiritual things in *The Da Vinci Code*. This passion for truth spurred us on in our efforts to answer their questions.

After he calls and encourages, God equips. He will make sure you are prepared and that you have the resources you need to carry out the work. The Spirit of the Lord came directly upon Gideon to strengthen him. The Pharaoh's daughter was divinely placed so that she could raise Moses, and then at the right time he could lead his people out of Egypt. Moses, before he died, laid hands on Joshua who received the spirit of wisdom. Esther was blessed with beauty and a mentor, the chief eunuch, who groomed her so that she could capture the King's favor in order to fulfill her role in saving the Jews.

One small example of how God equipped us to do our *Da Vinci Code* seminar took place when Gini traveled to Paris. At the time, she had read partway through *The Da Vinci Code.* Gini and her husband were exploring the city when they found themselves, by chance, in a beautiful church called Saint Sulpice. Later in the trip, as she continued to read the novel, she was surprised to find that Saint Sulpice plays a key role in *The Da Vinci Code*. God used that small incident to encourage us. And in a broader sense, God used our backgrounds and experiences to prepare us to put together the seminar and this book. Throughout this project, we both strongly felt God's call, experienced much fear, enjoyed his encouragement and reassurance, and were prepared and equipped to respond.

How is God calling you?

Are you willing to take the *Da Vinci Code* dare? Are you feeling the tug to use this book and movie as a way to share God's message of grace and truth? I hope so. It's a great opportunity to share the Good News, but it's not the only opportunity. Using *The Da Vinci Code* is not the only way to share your faith. Look for other open doors and use them.

Are you afraid? If so, that's okay. We were, too. Know that you are not alone. God himself is the Evangelist, "and we are merely colaborers in the sublime task. God essentially does the work. Jesus said, 'Apart from me, you can do nothing.' "[92] What a relief that we are not responsible for the results—we are merely witnesses. As long as you start climbing that hill, God will take over.

Do you need encouragement? Here's a promise, repeated three times, that you can claim. God spoke directly to Joshua: "Be strong and courageous . . . be strong and very courageous . . . have I not commanded you? Be strong and courageous. Do not be terrified; do not be discouraged, for the LORD your God will be with you wherever you go" (Josh. 1:6–9).

Are you equipped to share your faith? This book and many other resources exist to prepare and equip you to live out the Great Commission. It's important to study and practice the techniques and tools of evangelism. "Culture may provide us the opportunity to touch vast numbers of people, but we must still choose to endure the discipline of craftsmanship to seize the opportunity."[93] What steps can you take to prepare yourself to become a more effective witness?

The Da Vinci Code is a start; it provides a bridge to the culture, a place where we can meet, talk, answer questions, and share ourselves with those who need what we have. There is no more exciting place to be than where God is at work. He has used and will continue to use Dan Brown's story to call people to himself. Don't you want to be a part of that work? Take *The Da Vinci Code* dare. Ask God to use you. Yield yourself to his purposes and live out the call he's placed on your life. Don't be afraid. Start up the hill, and he will walk with you.

Our Prayer

God, thank you for your Word, which promises that you are with us. We know that with your strength and your courage, we can do whatever you call us to do. God, we are yours. Take away our fear and walk with us as we use *The Da Vinci Code*, and whatever other opportunities you give us, to share our faith. Amen.

APPENDIX

A

A Crash Course on *The Da Vinci Code*

Synopsis, characters, author

YOU MAY NOT have read *The Da Vinci Code.* Or perhaps it's been awhile and you would like to review the story. Maybe you have seen the movie and want to compare it to the book. In any case, we offer a brief synopsis of the novel, along with a character list and some information on author Dan Brown. Keep in mind that this appendix summarizes *The Da Vinci Code* and is not intended to serve as a critique of the novel's historical and theological ideas and claims. A caution: If you haven't yet read the book or seen the movie, reading the synopsis will reveal the plot twists and the ending.

Synopsis of the book

The Da Vinci Code details a two-thousand-year-old conspiracy that begins in Paris with the murder of the curator of the Louvre. The

Quick Facts on . . .

***The Da Vinci Code* novel**
Author: Dan Brown
Genre: Thriller
Date of first publication: March 2003
Publisher: Doubleday
Settings: The present day in Paris, France; Versailles, France; Vatican City; London, England; and the outskirts of Edinburgh, Scotland

***The Da Vinci Code* movie**
Director: Ron Howard
Producer: Brian Grazer
Screenwriter: Akiva Goldsman
Release Date: May 19, 2006
Studio: Columbia Pictures, Imagine Entertainment
Actors: Tom Hanks, Audrey Tatou, Ian McKellen, Jean Reno

Harvard code specialist called into the case pursues the culprit, and in so doing discovers an array of clues hidden in the works of Leonardo da Vinci. Thick with puzzles, symbols, cliff-hanging chapter endings, as well as plots by evil figures and secret societies, the novel reveals that Jesus was not divine, that he married the Mary Magdalene of the New Testament, had a child with her, that the bloodline survived in France, and that the church conspired for millennia to hide the truth. A key character announces among other things that the Roman emperor, Constantine, hatched the idea of Jesus' divinity as a political power play. Another revelation: the Holy Grail is not the cup Jesus drank from during the last supper; instead Mary Magdalene *is* the Holy Grail.

Plot summary

In the Louvre, an albino monk named Silas threatens curator Jacques Saunière with a gun, demanding to know where "it" is. Saunière tells him a carefully rehearsed lie before Silas shoots him and leaves him to die. The police awaken Robert Langdon, a symbology professor, asleep in his Paris hotel. An acquaintance of Saunière, he is suspected of the murder and is summoned to the Louvre for questioning. The police show him a photo of Saunière's body lying in the shape of a pentacle or five-pointed star. Saunière also drew a pentacle on his stomach with his own blood and left a secret message on the floor with a special black-light pen.

Meanwhile, after murdering Saunière, Silas calls the Teacher, a mysterious figure, with the information provided by Saunière—that the keystone is in the church of Saint Sulpice. Silas, a member of a strict Catholic organization called Opus Dei, straps on a studded belt called a cilice and whips himself bloody. Silas goes to Saint Sulpice and looks for the keystone but uncovers a dead end. Angry, he kills Sister Sandrine, the church caretaker affiliated with the Priory of Sion.

At the Louvre, Langdon meets Bezu Fache, a French police captain nicknamed "The Bull." Langdon explains that he and Saunière shared an interest in goddess iconography, the study of symbolism. Saunière's granddaughter, cryptologist Sophie Neveu, arrives and tells Langdon to call the embassy. Langdon calls the number and hears a message that warns him of danger and instructs him to meet Sophie in the bathroom.

Langdon meets Sophie and she throws a tracking device, planted by the French police, out the window and onto a moving vehicle. Sophie explains the meaning of the black-light pen message left by her grandfather: "P.S. Find Robert Langdon." The P.S. stands for Princess Sophie, Saunière's nickname for her. Langdon thinks P.S. might also mean Priory of Sion, the secret organization headed by Saunière, which is devoted to protecting the Holy Grail.

Langdon and Sophie find a key hidden by Saunière behind a Leonardo da Vinci painting called *Madonna of the Rocks*. The French police arrest Langdon, but Sophie rescues him by holding the painting hostage, and they escape the Louvre.

Sophie and Langdon travel to the Swiss bank that issued the key. Langdon tells Sophie more about the Priory of Sion and another group, the Knights Templar, explaining that the Priory protects secret documents connected to the Holy Grail.

Using the key to open a safety-deposit box at the bank, Sophie and Langdon find a cryptex, a puzzle box originally designed by Leonardo da Vinci and handmade by Saunière. The cryptex is password protected and cannot be opened. With the help of the bank manager, Sophie and Langdon escape the police with an armored car. Langdon realizes the cryptex is the keystone, the key to the Priory of Sion's secrets.

Sir Leigh Teabing, a historian, welcomes Sophie and Langdon to his castle where they go for refuge and for help opening the box. In an informal lecture to the pair, Teabing reveals that the Holy Grail is really Mary Magdalene who married Jesus and bore his children. He explains that the Bible didn't come straight from God but was compiled by Emperor Constantine. He also claims that Jesus' divinity was decided by a vote at Nicea. Teabing points out hidden symbols in Leonardo's *The Last Supper*. Teabing thinks Saunière was killed because the church did not want these secrets uncovered.

Silas appears and attacks Langdon, holds Sophie and Teabing at gunpoint, and demands the cryptex. Teabing and Sophie fight back, overpowering Silas. The police arrive, but Sophie, Langdon, Teabing, and his servant, Rémy, escape to England on Teabing's private plane, taking Silas with them. Unscrambling the writing on the cryptex, they realize the password is "Sofia." When they open the cryptex, however, they find another cryptex, with a clue about a tomb with a knight buried by a pope.

Fache tips off the British police, but Teabing outwits the police and the group escapes. Teabing goes with Sophie and Langdon to the

Temple Church in London to search for the tomb mentioned in the cryptex.

Set free by Rémy, who also follows the Teacher, Silas tails the group into the Temple Church. When he tries to get the cryptex from Langdon, the professor threatens to break it. Rémy takes Teabing hostage and forces Langdon to surrender the cryptex.

The police search Teabing's castle and find surveillance equipment used to spy on Saunière. By phone, the Teacher orders Silas to let Rémy have the cryptex. The Teacher kills Rémy in the park, then calls the police and turns in Silas. Police arrive at Opus Dei to arrest Silas. In a gun battle, Silas is shot, and he accidentally shoots Bishop Aringarosa. Silas dies. The Bishop survives but realizes that Teabing, who is the Teacher, has duped him.

Sophie and Langdon's research leads them to London's Westminster Abbey where they meet Teabing/the Teacher, who threatens them with a gun and reveals his plan to find the Grail himself.

Langdon figures out the password and opens the cryptex, secretly removing a roll of papyrus. Fache arrives and arrests Teabing.

The papyrus, which contains a poem from Saunière, leads Sophie and Langdon to Rosslyn Chapel, Scotland. There Sophie reunites with her long-lost brother and her grandmother, Marie Chauvel. She discovers that she truly is a descendant of Jesus and Mary Magdalene. Sophie and Langdon kiss and make plans to meet in Florence the next month. Back in Paris, Langdon continues to ponder the papyrus poem. He finally decides that the poem points to the final resting place of Mary Magdalene, also known as the Holy Grail; her bones are entombed beneath the point of the glass pyramid at the Louvre. He visits the spot and falls to his knees in reverence.

Characters

Manuel Aringarosa. Bishop of Opus Dei, a Catholic organization that values strict self-discipline.

Marie Chauvel. Saunière's wife and Sophie's grandmother. Chauvel lives in a cottage near Rosslyn Chapel, Scotland, with her grandson, Sophie's long-lost brother.

Bezu Fache. Captain of the French Judicial Police and nicknamed "The Bull." Fache pursues Langdon and Sophie through England, France, and Scotland as he tries to solve Saunière's murder.

Robert Langdon. The story's hero, Langdon is a professor of symbology at Harvard. He and Sophie fall in love as they chase down clues and solve puzzles in a whirlwind search for the Holy Grail.

Rémy Legaludec. Sir Leigh Teabing's servant. Legaludec secretly works for the Teacher and gets involved in the plot to recover the Grail.

Sophie Neveu. A cryptologist with the French Judicial Police. The heroine of the novel and movie, Sophie works with Langdon to crack the mystery of Jacques Saunière's Priory of Sion involvement. Sophie is the granddaughter of Saunière and Marie Chauvel and a descendant of Jesus and Mary Magdalene.

Sister Sandrine. Nun who acts as caretaker of the Church of Saint Sulpice. She guards a clue to the search for the Grail. Sister Sandrine is murdered by Silas.

Jacques Saunière. Curator at the Louvre, Saunière is murdered there by Silas. Before he dies, he leaves several clues for Sophie, his granddaughter. A descendant of Jesus and Mary Magdalene, Saunière secretly heads the Priory of Sion, a secret organization that protects the Grail.

Silas. An albino monk affiliated with Opus Dei, Silas murders Jacques Saunière. Obsessed with self-punishment, Silas serves Bishop Aringarosa and someone he calls "The Teacher," a mysterious figure who turns out to be Sir Leigh Teabing.

Leigh Teabing. The villain of the novel, Sir Leigh Teabing is a knight and a Royal Historian. Crippled by polio, Teabing's passion is the search for the Holy Grail. He takes on an alter ego, the Teacher, who resorts to murder.

Author

Dan Brown is a graduate of Amherst College and Phillips Exeter Academy. He spent time as an English teacher before publishing his first novel in 1996, *Digital Fortress.* Other novels written by Brown include *Angels and Demons* and *Deception Point.* According to his Web site, Brown's interests include codebreaking, covert government agencies, and secret organizations. Wife Blythe, an art historian and painter, collaborates on his research and accompanies him on his frequent research trips. A quote from Dan Brown on religion: "I consider myself a student of many religions. The more I learn, the more questions I have. For me, the spiritual quest will be a life-long work in progress."[1] His best-selling novel, *The Da Vinci Code*, begins with the statement: "All descriptions of artwork, architecture, documents, and secret rituals in this novel are accurate." This opening statement has sparked much controversy, because much of the history in the novel is, in fact, inaccurate. Could Brown's statement itself be part of the fiction?

1. Dan Brown.com, "Common Questions," www.danbrown.com, http://www.danbrown.com/novels/davinci_code/faqs.html (accessed 2/25/05).

APPENDIX

B

Who Were the Gnostics?

By W. Ward Gasque, PhD

Dr. W. Ward Gasque is an historian of early Christianity with a PhD from Manchester University, England. He studied under the late Professor F. F. Bruce, perhaps the most distinguished Bible scholar of the second half of the twentieth century. An authority on The Acts of the Apostles (the earliest history of the first-century church) and the writings of Saint Paul (the oldest documents contained in the New Testament), he is the author of two books, editor of four collections of essays, and also editor of more than twenty commentaries. Plus, he has written more than two hundred articles and numerous book reviews for publications such as Christianity Today, Christian Week, Interpretation, Theologische Zeitschrift, Hokmah, Radix, *and* Themelios.

* * *

DAN Brown's novel, *The Da Vinci Code*, refers to Gnostics and to certain ancient documents produced by this somewhat amorphous group of pre-Christians and early Christian heretics. Gnostics believed that matter is evil and redemption is attained by an enlightened elite through esoteric religious experience.

A cache of these writings, written originally in Greek but translated into Coptic (the language spoken by Egyptian Christians historically) was discovered in 1945 near the village of Nag Hammadi, Egypt. These have been translated into English and annotated by scholars, and are popularly known as "The Nag Hammadi Library" (see appendix C).

In *The Da Vinci Code*, these documents are misleadingly called "the earliest Christian records" (p. 245); in fact, the earliest Greek originals of any of these documents are dated at least a century later than the latest New Testament writings. The Coptic versions date from the fourth century.

The word *Gnostic* comes from *gnosis*, the Greek word for "knowledge." The term is applied to a wide range of ancient writings and groups, much as the term *New Age* is used today. *The Da Vinci Code* refers to a number of these ancient documents and suggests that they preserved the earlier view of Christianity, namely, that Jesus was truly human. The fact is quite the opposite: the Gnostic writings deny the true humanity of Jesus, and it is the New Testament writings that affirm his humanity!

Gnostic ideas are still alive in our culture today. Madame Blavatsky, the nineteenth-century founder of Theosophy, promoted various Gnostic themes, as have many twentieth-century New Age gurus. Gnostic churches can be found in many North American cities and in Europe, as well as popular writers who seem to find Gnostic themes attractive. Check out your local general bookstores, such as Borders or Barnes & Noble, and you will likely find as many books promoting Gnosticism as traditional Christianity.

Frequently Asked Questions (FAQs) on the Gnostics

Q. Who were the Gnostics?

A. The traditional answer is that they were early Christian heretics who rejected such doctrines as the true humanity of Jesus, his atoning death and resurrection, the inspiration of the Hebrew Bible (the Old Testament), and, indeed, the goodness of the created world. Simon of Samaria, mentioned in the Acts of the Apostles (chapter 8), is identified as a Gnostic by early Christian writers, though the New Testament describes him merely as a magician or sorcerer. Other early Gnostics were Menander and Saturninus of Syrian Antioch, Cerinthus of Asia Minor, Basilides of Egypt, Marcion of Pontus, Valentinus of Alexandria and Rome, as well as other second-century teachers.

More recently, scholars have concluded that Gnosticism is broader than a post-Christian heresy. Rather, it represents a religious-philosophical ethos that permeated the Graeco-Roman world (and beyond) in the earliest Christian centuries. These ideas influenced people connected with the earliest Christian communities, but they were held and developed by many who had no contact with the church. No evidence exists that these ideas influenced the development of earliest Christianity, nor influenced any of the disciples of Jesus of the first generation (as implied by *The Da Vinci Code*).

Q. What is the underlying theme or message of Gnostic writings?

A. Gnostics believe they have certain knowledge revealed only to those who have received secret (esoteric) teaching. This teaching may come through a heavenly or spiritual being or through a man (or, in some cases, a woman) who has received this knowledge by special revelation. Fundamental to Gnostic theology is a radical cosmological dualism, an opposition between the heavenly or spiritual world and the material world, which is evil.

The problem of sin for Gnostics is related to our physical existence. They view the material world as evil through and through. Salvation is to be sought by an escape from this material world and absorption into the spiritual world through a rejection of things related to the body (*soma*) and soul (*psyche*) in favor of spirit (*pneuma*). In contrast to the Christian doctrines of the physical world being created by the supreme God and the hope of salvation in a resurrected body, Gnostics regard the physical world as the result of either (1) a tragic cosmic accident (or fall), or (2) the creation of an evil god. Salvation is sought by an escape from the body.

The idea of an incarnation of God (as in the New Testament) or salvation by suffering (the cross of Christ) is anathema to a Gnostic. A huge variety of Gnostic ideas exist, but Christian Gnostics believe that sparks of divinity have been encapsulated within certain spiritual (pneumatic) individuals. God sent his Redeemer (Christ) to awaken them to their divine potential and to assist them in their attempt to escape the prison of the body and the physical world. This he does by means of secret teaching that enables Gnostics to transcend the physical world in which they currently live and eventually to escape through death. They then traverse the planetary spheres ruled over by hostile demons and, if they are lucky, become reunited with the God who is pure Spirit ("the All" or "Fullness," Greek *pleroma*).

Q. Do the Gnostics still exist?

A. Yes, many different Gnostic and Gnostic-like groups are active today, though they have no real continuity historically with the Gnosticism of the first through the fourth centuries other than being attracted to their writings and doctrines.

For example, there is a First Gnostic Church of Cypress, California (http://www.1gnostic.com/), and the Gnostic Church of Saint Mary Magdalene (http://magdalene.wise1.com/index.html), which may be located only on the World Wide Web (WWW).

On a visit to Toronto some months ago, I searched the Web and found at least four distinct Gnostic Churches in that city. None, apparently, fellowships with the others.

The Gnostic Society of Los Angeles has its own bishop and is located at 3363 Glendale Avenue, Los Angeles, CA 90003. Their Web site, http://gnosis.org/gnostsoc/gnostsoc.htm, gives a clear picture of their understanding of their history and distinctive doctrines.

The majority of New Age religious and semi-religious groups has been influenced by basic Gnostic ideas, beginning with Theosophy.

Q. What is so attractive about Gnostic beliefs?

A. Few people are attracted to the hard-core Gnosticism rooted in the historical Gnostic texts. The Gnostic congregations are very small, comparable in size to the Seventh-Day Baptists. But a variety of writers, speakers, and nontraditional healers select Gnostic phrases and concepts and dress them up in contemporary Western garb to present them as newly discovered or recovered truth; few of their hearers bother to check the primary sources for context. For example, we are told that the Gnostics were protofeminists (Mary [Magdalene] is very prominent in a few Gnostic texts), and yet the most famous Gnostic document, the *Gospel of Thomas*, concludes with Jesus saying that "every woman who will make herself male will enter the kingdom of heaven" (Logion 114). This doesn't sound like women's liberation to me!

What many people find attractive is the spin that some contemporary writers have put on Gnosticism rather than the thing itself. It's like the woman in Leonardo's *Last Supper*: she's just not there! Naïve and gullible readers who are historically illiterate believe what they are told by people who write books and give lectures, when a little firsthand investigation would demonstrate the truth.

Anyone interested in finding out more about Gnosticism should read the primary documents, easily accessible via any good university or college library or via the Internet.

Q. What are the Gnostic views of Jesus, the crucifixion, and the resurrection?

A. Among the Gnostics, Jesus is a god/spirit/redeemer who has come to dispel the darkness of our ignorance by revealing the truth. He comes to only a select few, because only a few have within them the spark of divinity.

The Gnostic perspective on Jesus is totally different from the outlook of the New Testament; Jesus was not crucified; he did not die; and therefore there is no need for a resurrection. Different writers worked this out theologically in a wide variety of ways.

Q. In *The Da Vinci Code*, Professor Teabing claims that more than eighty gospels were considered for the New Testament, but only four were chosen (p. 231). Is this true?

A. No. First, there are not eighty documents labeled "gospels" among all of the literature of the first four Christian centuries, and then there was no formal process of sifting through the alternative versions that Teabing's claim suggests.

There were no competing first-century gospels to be considered as alternatives to the Gospels of Matthew, Mark, Luke, and John, as far as we have any evidence. Originally, these four documents circulated independently but seemed to have been regarded as authoritative by churches in different regions of the Roman Empire. But sometime toward the middle of the second century, they were brought together as a group and linked with the letters of Paul and most (but not all) of the writings that came to make up the Greek New Testament.

While it is true that there was some debate concerning the extent of the canon (the collection of documents to be included in the Christian Bible), the debate was over a limited number of New Testament books (Hebrews, James, 2 Peter, 2 and 3 John, Jude, Revelation), none of them Gospels.

The other writings called "gospels" are one, two, three, four, and more centuries later than the four canonical Gospels. And numerous so-called "gospels" continue to be written and then "discovered" in our times, very much like the "Secret Files" related to the bogus "Priory of Sion" that were forged and then slipped into the National Library of France by Pierre Plantard and his associates.

Q. Why were the Gnostic writings ignored when the New Testament was being put together? Do the Gnostic writings belong in the Bible?

A. There is no evidence that any of the Gnostic documents in the Nag Hammadi Library or any other collection was ever widely recognized as authoritative. It is debatable whether they were regarded as "holy scripture" even within the groups where they were read. But their rejection of the Old Testament (not to mention the God of the Jewish people) and its teachings (for example, its teaching about creation), their denial of the true humanity of Christ and his suffering for humankind, and their esoteric doctrines that were so contrary to the spirit and the letter of both the Old Testament and the New Testament, caused them to be condemned as heretical by the majority of Christians. There is no evidence that anyone ever made an attempt to get any of these writings added to the Bible.

Q. How do the Gnostic writings compare to the New Testament Gospels of Matthew, Mark, Luke, and John?

A. The New Testament Gospels have a historical context. Jesus lives in Roman Palestine. He has a mother, a lineage, a heritage, an occupation; he walks the dusty roads, teaching and healing. From one-quarter to one-half of the narrative of each of the canonical Gospels is taken up with Jesus' passion, namely, his last trip to Jerusalem, his arrest, trial, and crucifixion, followed by his resurrection.

None of this is contained in the Gnostic gospels. Jesus' and his disciples' revelatory teaching in the Gnostic gospels has no context. It is as if Jesus were a ghost or a spirit or perhaps a philosopher like Socrates (though spouting some fairly bizarre teachings).

Q. Are Gnostic writings accurate and reliable? How many copies exist?

A. No. There are only a handful. If not for the discovery of the Nag Hammadi sixty years ago, we would not know of the existence of many of these documents.

Q. What was the early church's opinion of Gnosticism? Were the Gnostics considered Christians?

A. The main body of the church regarded Gnostics as heretics, people who believed and taught false doctrine that undermined the true gospel of Jesus Christ. The leading pagan thinkers of the day, the so-called Neo-Platonists, also considered them as "heretics." They were not considered to be either good Christians or clear thinkers. Of course, many of them who had some connection to the church believed themselves Christians, possibly the *only* Christians.

Q. What is the Gnostic view of women? Did the Gnostics write about the sacred feminine?

A. Gnostics have a mixed review in regard to their views of women. Some texts suggest that women had a lot of freedom and might even be teachers; others suggest very negative views of women (and especially of sexuality, whether male or female), as in the quotation from the *Gospel of Thomas*, mentioned before. Of course, the same can be said of what developed into Orthodox Christianity. While Jesus never said a word to suggest that women were anything less than full members of his community of disciples, and Paul (in spite of his bad press to the contrary) affirmed women in the exercise of whatever gifts they had been given by the Lord, the later church tended to have a more guarded view of the role of women in the church.

No, the Gnostics never wrote about the sacred feminine. This is a creation of Dan Brown's fiction.

Q. Do the Gnostic writings prove that Mary Magdalene was the wife of Jesus? (*The Da Vinci Code*, p. 246)

A. No. *The Gospel of Philip*, quoted by Teabing, does not suggest that Jesus was married to Mary Magdalene. There are two references to Mary Magdalene as being the "companion" of Jesus. Teabing says that the Aramaic word for "companion" really means spouse. Two things are wrong with this: (1) *The Gospel of Philip* was originally written not in Aramaic but in Greek and exists only in Coptic. The word in the Coptic manuscript is a Greek loanword, related to the well-known *koinonia* (fellowship). It means "companion," "friend," or "associate," not spouse, and (2) There is no corresponding word in Aramaic that could mean spouse.

Further, the reference to Jesus' kissing Mary (whether "on the lips" or "on the cheek"—there is a gap in the text, so it is unclear where he kissed her) has no sexual connotation in societies where people frequently kiss family members and close friends, of both sexes, when they greet one another (as in Italy, France, the Middle East, and parts of Canada). Remember the New Testament text: "Greet all the brothers [and sisters] with a holy kiss" (1 Thess. 5:26).

There is no reference in any Gnostic text, any apocryphal gospel, or any other ancient writing to suggest that Jesus was married. Nor did anyone ever suggest this prior to the second half of the twentieth century, when a Presbyterian minister who taught at a small church college began to write books on Jesus' sexuality. None of the legendary traditions about Mary Magdalene from the Middle Ages on have ever suggested that she was married to Jesus. And it is not true that all devout Jewish men were married (the Essenes, who were ultra-devout, eschewed marriage; and Paul, a very prominent and devout Jew, was not married).

The earliest and most reliable tradition about Mary Magdalene was that she went with the apostle John to Ephesus, along with Mary the mother of Jesus, and became John's wife. But this is uncertain.

Q. Were the Gnostic writings suppressed or hidden by the Vatican, as suggested by Professor Teabing in *The Da Vinci Code* (p. 234)?

A. This is one of the many anachronisms in Dan Brown's book. First, Vatican did not become the headquarters for the Catholic Church in Rome until the eleventh century, so documents would not have been suppressed by "the Vatican" in the fourth century. Secondly, the Bishop of Rome had little influence over the churches in the East at this time. If anybody suppressed any documents in, say, Egypt or Syria, it would have been the Bishop of Alexandria or the Bishop of Antioch. Perhaps the monastery librarian purged books so as to make room for other, presumably better, books much as contemporary librarians do. In fact, evidence exists that the Bishop of Alexandria suppressed these documents around the time that the codices (now called the Nag Hammadi Library) were buried—not because they had any hidden secrets but because they were regarded as heretical. But now we have them, and you can read them for yourself.

Q. Where can I read more about Gnosticism?

For further reading, see appendix C.

APPENDIX

C

For Further Reading . . .

. . . on *The Da Vinci Code*

Breaking the Da Vinci Code, Darrell L. Bock, PhD (Nelson)
Cracking Da Vinci's Code, James L. Garlow & Peter Jones (Victor)
The Da Vinci Code, Gnostic Gospels & the Gospel, W. Ward Gasque, PhD (Regent College Audio)
The Da Vinci Deception, Erwin W. Lutzer (Tyndale)

. . . on sharing your faith

a.k.a. "Lost": Discovering Ways to Connect with the People Jesus Misses Most, Jim Henderson (Waterbrook)
The Case for Christ, Lee Strobel (Zondervan)
The Case for Faith, Lee Strobel (Zondervan)
Get the Word Out: How God Shapes and Sends His Witnesses, John Teter (InterVarsity)
Going Public with Your Faith: Becoming a Spiritual Influence at Work, William Carr Peel, ThM & Walt Larimore, MD (Zondervan)
Permission Evangelism: When to Talk, When to Walk, Michael L. Simpson (NexGen)
Questioning Evangelism, Randy Newman (Kregel)

. . . on overcoming fear

Boundaries Face to Face: How to Have That Difficult Conversation You've Been Avoiding, Dr. Henry Cloud & Dr. John Townsend (Zondervan)

If You Want to Walk on Water, You've Got to Get Out of the Boat, John Ortberg (Zondervan)

Scaling the Wall: Overcoming Obstacles to Missions Involvement, Kathy Hicks (Gabriel)

. . . on the Gnostics (the following books and articles are recommended by W. Ward Gasque, PhD)

1. Primary texts

Robinson, James M., et al. *The Coptic Gnostic Library: A Complete Edition of the Nag Hammadi Codices*, 11 vols. (Leiden: Brill, 1975–95). Complete translations with notes and commentary.

Robinson, James M., ed. *The Nag Hammadi Library in English* (San Francisco: Harper San Francisco, 1988).

http://www.gnosis.org/library.html. Web site of The Gnostic Society Library, which contains translations of all of the Nag Hammadi texts plus many other primary documents relating to the Gnostics, as well as important secondary literature.

2. Articles offering compact overviews of subject and modern research (with extensive bibliographies)

Scholer, David M. "Gnosis, Gnosticism," in *Dictionary of the Later New Testament and Its Development*, ed. Ralph P. Martin and Peter H. Davids (Downers Grove: InterVarsity Press, 1999), 400–12.

Yamauchi, Edwin M. "Gnosticism," in *Dictionary of New Testament Background*, ed., Craig A. Evans and Stanley E. Porter (Downers Grove: InterVarsity Press, 2000), 414–18.

Yamauchi, Edwin M. "Gnosis, Gnosticism," in *Dictionary of Paul and His Letters*, ed. Gerald F. Hawthorne, Ralph P. Martin, and Daniel G. Reid (Downers Grove: InterVarsity Press, 1993), 350–54.

3. For further reading

Filoramo, Giovanni. *A History of Gnosticism* (Oxford: Blackwell, 1990). An illuminating and helpful introduction to the topic by an Italian historian.

Grant, Robert M. *Gnosticism and Early Christianity*, rev. ed. (New York: Harper & Row, 1966). A useful introduction by a distinguished University of Chicago historian.

Jonas, Hans. *The Gnostic Religion,* second ed. (Boston: Beacon Press, 1963). A classical and accessible introduction to some of the major documents and ideas of Gnosticism in the broadest sense.

Wilson, R. McL. *Gnosis and the New Testament* (Oxford: Blackwell, 1968). An authoritative and balanced treatment of the relationship of Gnosticism/Gnosis to earliest Christianity by one of the prime translators of the Nag Hammadi texts.

APPENDIX

D

Five Steps to Prepare for Sharing Your Faith

1. Begin your day by spending at least fifteen minutes with God. Tell him specifically what you love about him today. Tell how you messed up yesterday and apologize. He is just and forgives us for all our sins through Jesus' shed blood (1 John 1:7–9). Thank him for your salvation. Then, read at least ten consecutive verses from your Bible. Ask God to teach you what you'll need for today. Read them again. Be quiet and listen. He will point out something from the Bible just for you. Write it down to carry with you today. Ask him to please use you today. Wait. He's there. You'll probably feel his closeness, have some new thoughts about him, or hear his Word in your mind.
2. As you shower, think back over the answers to the question: "Could Jesus have been married?" Someone might ask that today. Which one of the eight reasons will you use to prove that Jesus wasn't married?
3. As you eat your breakfast, find the Bible verse for the reason you chose. Write it down on the other side of God's verse for you today.

4. As you grab your *Da Vinci Code* book and your keys, remind yourself that you asked God to use you today. He will. Remember, it won't be you who will do the work, it's the Father.
5. Keep your eyes open. Watch people carefully. Be friendly. Give them a chance to see your book cover. Ask someone who grins at your book, "Have you read it? What did you think?"

They'll answer. Then if they ask you your opinion, take the reins and ride. You might start out like this: "It was interesting, but I don't think Jesus could have really been married because . . ." Give your answer with a verse reference so they can read it for themselves. Then see what God will do through you. God can use even your five-minute chat!

For additional information, see the authors' Web site:

www.fearnotdavinci.com

Notes

1. BBC News, "Da Vinci Code Video Game Planned," www.news.bbc.co.uk, http://news.bbc.co.uk/2/hi/entertainment/4403636.stm (accessed 11/8/05).

2. Paris Muse, "Cracking *The Da Vinci Code*," www.parismuse.com, http://www.parismuse.com/about/news/da-vinci-code.shtml (accessed 11/8/05).

3. British Tours LTD, "See the London Sights Featured in Dan Brown's Bestselling Novel *The Da Vinci Code*," www.britishtours.com, http://www.britishtours.com/davincicodetours.html (accessed 11/8/05).

4. Chateau de Villette, "Da Vinci Code Tours," www.frenchvacations.com, http://www.frenchvacation.com/daVinciCodeTour.htm (accessed 11/8/05).

5. Beyond Boundaries, "On the Trail of *The Da Vinci Code,*" www.beyondboundariestravel.com, http://www.beyondboundariestravel.com/davinci.html (accessed 11/8/05).

6. Sacred Journeys For Women, "Da Vinci Pilgrimage," www.sacredjourneys.com, http://www.sacredjourneys.com/davinci.html (accessed 11/8/05).

7. CNN.com, "Nun Confronts Hanks Over *Da Vinci Code,*" www.cnn.com, http://www.cnn.com/2005/WORLD/europe/08/16/davinci.protest/ (accessed 11/8/05).

8. Dennis Ladaw, "Why Bea Alonzo Refuses to Read *The Da Vinci Code*," www.abs-cbnnews.com, www.abs-cbnnews.com/storypage.aspx?StoryId=20349 (accessed 10/28/05).

9. Hollywood Reporter, "*Da Vinci Code* Unlocked for Video Games," www.msnbc.msn.com, http://msnbc.msn.com/id/9925376/ (accessed 11/9/05).

10. Sweet Briar College, "Da Vinci's Code," www.sbc.edu, http://witcombe.sbc.edu/davincicode/magdalen-sacred-feminine.html (accessed 11/9/05).

11. Jane Franklin Hall, University of Tasmania, "The Da Vinci Code," www.utas.edu, http://www.utas.edu.au/docs/jane_franklin_hall/summerschool.htm (accessed 11/9/05).

12. Newbattle Abbey College, "A Cracking Course for Fans of Da Vinci Code," www.newbattleabbeycollege.co.uk, http://www.newbattleabbeycollege.co.uk/news_details.asp?NewsID=9 (accessed 11/9/05).

13. Louisiana Scholars' College, Northwestern State University, "The Da Vinci Code," www.nsula.edu, http://www.nsula.edu/news/davin07.htm (accessed 11/9/05).

14. The Barna Group, "Religious Books Attract a Diverse Audience Dominated by Women and Boomers," www.barna.org, http://www.barna.org/FlexPage.aspx?Page=BarnaUpdate&BarnaUpdateID=191 (accessed 6/30/05).

15. David Mehegan, "Thriller Instinct" (*Boston Globe*, 5/8/04).

16. Amy Welborn, *De-coding Da Vinci* (Huntington, Indiana: Our Sunday Visitor, 2004), 20.

17. Darrell L. Bock, PhD, "The Good News of Da Vinci," *Christianity Today* (January, 2004), 62.

18. Deborah Caldwell, "Unpacking The Code," www.beliefnet.com, http://www.beliefnet.com/story/167/story_16783.html (accessed 6/24/05).

19. Darrell L. Bock, PhD, *Breaking the Da Vinci Code* (Nashville: Nelson Books, 2004), 6.

20. Cathleen Falsani, "The Next Great Awakening?" (*Chicago Sun-Times*, 3/18/04).

21. Hank Hanegraaff and Paul L. Maier, *The Da Vinci Code: Fact or Fiction?* (Wheaton, Illinois: Tyndale House, 2004), 68.

22. Michael L. Simpson, *Permission Evangelism* (Colorado Springs, Colorado: NexGen/Cook Communications, 2003), 128.

23. John Teter, *Get the Word Out: How God Shapes and Sends His Witnesses* (Downers Grove, Illinois: InterVarsity Press, 2003), 78.

24. Lewis A. Drummond, *Reaching Generation Next: Effective Evangelism in Today's Culture* (Grand Rapids, Michigan: Baker, 2002), 113.

25. Jim Henderson, *a.k.a. Lost: Discovering Ways to Connect with the People Jesus Misses Most* (Colorado Springs, Colorado: Waterbrook, 2005), 11.

26. Bret Johnson, *Bret Johnson Devotional* (www.bretjohnsondevotional@yahoogroups.com, 11/2/05).

27. Jim Henderson, 142.

28. Henderson, 61.

29. William Carr Peel, ThM, and Walt Larimore, MD, *Going Public with Your Faith: Becoming a Spiritual Influence at Work* (Grand Rapids, Michigan: Zondervan, 2003), 26–27.

30. Michael L. Simpson, *Permission Evangelism* (Colorado Springs, Colorado: NexGen, 2003), 49.

31. Peel, *Going Public with Your Faith.*

32. Simpson, 16–17.

33. Simpson, 168.

34. Peel, *Going Public with Your Faith*, 21.

35. Revelation 21:5 NKJV.

36. Brian Hill and Dee Power, "From 17 Full Grown Elephants? That's a Lot of Books," www.brianhillanddeepower.com, http://www.brianhillanddeepower.com/17elephants.html (accessed 10/30/05).

37. Peel, *Going Public with Your Faith*, 134.

38. Dan Brown, *The Da Vinci Code* (New York: Doubleday, 2003), 120.

39. Brown, 120.

40. Brown, 120.

41. Brown, 121.

42. Brown, 121.

43. Brown, 95.

44. SCALA. *Leonardo Da Vinci*, Amilcare Pizzi S.p.A, Cinisello Balsame (Milan: SCALA Group S.p.A, 1990).

45. Brown, 243.

46. Sherwin B. Nuland, "Inside the Mind of a Genius: Secrets of the Da Vinci Code," *U.S. News and World Report Special Edition* (Feb. 2005).

47. Robert Wallace and the Editors of Time-Life Books, *The World of Leonardo: 1452–1519* (Time Inc., 1966).

48. Margaret Atwood, "That Certain Thing Called the Girlfriend" (*New York Times Books*, 5/11/86), http://www.nytimes.com/books/00/09/03/specials/atwood-girlfriend.html (accessed 11/9/05).

49. Merriam Webster Online Dictionary, www.m-w.com, http://www.m-w.com/cgi-bin/dictionary?book=Dictionary&va=holy (accessed 8/07/05).

50. Tom Holladay and Kay Warren, *Foundations: Participant's Guide* (Grand Rapids, Michigan: Zondervan, 2003), 46.

51. Holladay, 111. See also Matthew 26:46; Luke 13:3; Romans 6:23.

52. Chuck Colson, *Answers to Your Kids' Questions* (Wheaton, Illinois: Tyndale, 2000), 113.

53. John Eldredge, *Wild at Heart* (Nashville, Tennessee: Thomas Nelson, 2001), 180.

54. Brown, 231.

55. Brown, 232.

56. Brown, 232.

57. John F. MacArthur, Jr., *Take God's Word for It* (Glendale: G/L Publications, 1980), 588–63.

58. MacArthur, 64.

59. *The Infancy Gospel of Thomas,* "The Apocryphal New Testament," The Gnostic Society Library (Oxford: Clarendon Press, 1924), www.gnosis.org/library/inftoma.htm.

60. *Gospel of Thomas*, Nag Hammadi Library. The Gnostic Society Library. www.gnosis.org/naghamm/thomas poxy.htm.

61. *Gospel of Philip*, Nag Hammadi Library. www.gnosis.org/naghamm/gop.htm.

62. Erwin Lutzer, *The Da Vinci Deception* (Wheaton, Illinois: Tyndale Audio, 2004).

63. Lutzer.

64. MacArthur, 62.

65. Lutzer.

66. MacArthur, 65.

67. Orville E. Daniel, *A Harmony of the Four Gospels* (Grand Rapids, Michigan: Baker, 1996).

68. Daniel, 68–76.

69. Brown, 244.

70. Charles R. Swindoll, general editor. *The Living Insights Study Bible, New International Version* (Grand Rapids, Michigan: Zondervan, 1996), 1004.

71. Brown, 248–249.

72. Brown, 234.

73. Brown, 231–235.

74. Brown, 247.

75. Brown, 341.

76. Brown, 342.

77. Wayne Martindale and Jerry Root, eds., *The Quotable Lewis* (Wheaton, Illinois: Tyndale, 1989) 444.

78. *Gospel of Thomas.*

79. James Garlow and Peter Jones, *Cracking Da Vinci's Code* (Colorado Springs: Cook, 2004).

80. Hanegraaff, 43.

81. Erwin Lutzer, *The Da Vinci Deception* (Wheaton, Illinois: Tyndale Audio, 2004).

82. Lutzer.

83. Garlow and Jones.

84. Apologetics Index, "Apologetics Index-G: an apologetics index research resource," www.apologeticsindex.org, http://www.apologeticsindex.org/g00.html, (accessed 1/14/05).

85. Bock, 68.

86. Isenberg and Robinson, eds., "Secrets of the Da Vinci Code" (*U.S. News & World Report*, February 22, 2005).

87. Verses we memorized: John 1:12; John 3:16–18; John 10:10; John 14:6; Romans 3:23; Romans 5:8; Romans 6:23; 1 Corinthians 15:3, 4; Ephesians 2:8–9; Hebrews 13:5; 1 John 4:11–13; Revelation 3:20.

88. John 10:10 NASB.

89. Daniel.

90. John Ortberg, *If You Want to Walk on Water, You've Got to Get Out of the Boat* (Grand Rapids, Michigan: Zondervan, 2001), 118.

91. Ortberg, 9.

92. Lewis A. Drummond, *Reaching Generation Next: Effective Evangelism in Today's Culture* (Grand Rapids, Michigan: Baker Books, 2002), 114.